CURRENCY AND BANKING.

BY

BONAMY PRICE,

PROFESSOR OF POLITICAL ECONOMY IN THE UNIVERSITY OF OXFORD.

NEW YORK:
D. APPLETON AND COMPANY,
549 AND 551 BROADWAY.
1876.

PREFACE.

THIS work is founded on the view of Currency and Banking taken in the Lectures on the Principles of Currency, delivered at Oxford, and published in 1869, and also in other writings. I have met with no reason which, in my opinion, requires that the views therein expressed should be altered.

CONTENTS.

CURRENCY AND BANKING.

CHAPTER I.

METALLIC CURRENCY.

To commence an investigation of the principles of currency is to enter a region which may be justly described as chaos. The very sound of the word currency makes a man turn his back or shut his ears; his immediate instinct is to fly from a subject with which he associates such unendurable jargon. To obtain clear, definite, and intelligible knowledge in currency almost seems to be a task exceeding the powers of the human intellect. "There was no need," exclaimed recently an Ex-Lord Mayor in the House of Commons, "to go into all the deeper quagmires of bank-notes and such things, which no man could understand in this world, or, as he believed, in the next." Yet what is currency but one of man's own inventions, a contrivance which he has himself devised for rendering an indespensable service to the practical life of every civilized people? It is easy to conceive that the most familiar natural objects should possess secrets which no research nor acuteness can explore; the meanest plant and the humblest animal inexorably refuse to reveal what life is. But that machinery expressly invented by man himself to accomplish any obvious purpose—that tools which men constructed at the dawn of civilization, and which are now at work every hour and in every country—that the action of such instruments should be incomprehensible to man's reason is assuredly a most astonishing marvel. And what increases the wonder is the certain fact that it is of vital importance to every nation to solve correctly the questions of currency. A bad currency, as experience has only too often shown, inflicts severe calamities on a nation; loss and ruin, public and private, all history teaches, are the deadly arrows which an ill-constructed currency carries in its quiver. Thus every kind of political and social motive calls for the right understanding of a tool which is in every man's hand, and yet, if we may judge from the floods of speaking and writing which have been poured forth about it, what money is and does, what is a sound and what a bad money, how it works, what effects it has and what it has not, are matters absolutely undiscoverable.

This failure, had it been inevitable, would have constituted the most wonderful enigma in the history of the human mind; but it is neither necessary nor real. Currency can be easily and naturally explained if only men choose that it shall be. It is the one subject which mortals refuse to study. Every man thinks himself qualified to lay down rules concerning it, but without any sense of responsibility of first learning what it is. Thus currency has become the prey of every kind of arbitrary and ignorant assumption. In other subjects men know that they must not speak about them until they have mastered them by systematic study; but every one thinks himself fit to dogmatise off-hand on currency. And who are the persons who inevitably come to the front as leaders under such circumstances? The practical men, those who make large fortunes by handling these tools: who so likely to know all about them? But do great bankers and bill-brokers study currency? Have they, generally, any conception of disciplined and methodical investigation of the real nature of the operations they carry on? Do they follow the road of all true science, and analyse down to first principles? Had such been the course pursued by so-called authorities, currency would not be in the mire of confusion where we find it to-day. To extemporise dogma is far easier; just as great astronomical authorities laid down, as the first principle of their science, that the planets moved in circles, for God Almighty would not suffer them to revolve in any but perfect curves.

True science alone is clear: and there is but one road to true science, a thorough analysis of all the facts and elements of a subject. With this law must be combined another—a firm determination to accept all that analysis teaches, and resolutely to reject all that is inconsistent with it. This last rule is of supreme importance in currency. No one accepts calculations which contradict the multiplication table; in currency the common practice is to have no multiplication table, to lay down no first principle to which every doctrine must be referred. The absence of any effort to establish logical connection between new utterances and previously established conclusions is the peculiar misfortune of currency. Let us then eschew *à priori* and gratuitous theory, the theory of the great City practical man, the man of money; let us seek, as others seek, that carefully co-ordinated science, founded on the facts yielded by analysis, which alone constitutes true knowledge.

We now proceed with our investigation. We seek to discover the motive, the action, and the laws of currency. But the word currency is an abstract term, a generic expression; we must begin with the concrete, before we can sum up and generalise in an abstract formula. We must go to another word, money, for our starting point. Diverse meanings are loosely given to this word, many inconsistent with each other; so that to say that currency is money would throw no light upon our path. Fortunately, however, there is a sense of the word money which no one disputes, which is recognised by the whole world. Whatever else may or may not be money, coin, at any rate, is money; and coin is a definite, concrete, substance. The derivation itself of the word proclaims the fact: it comes from Juno Moneta, whose temple was the mint in which Roman coin was made, the stamped pieces of metal which constituted the currency of Rome. Thus the word money implies minting, that is, the shaping and stamping those bits of metal which are employed in buying and selling. Here we are on solid ground: we have an objective substance which it is our business to analyse, as to what it is and what it does; every logical consequence we obtain from it we may rely on with perfect safety. No one denies that coin is true and complete money; what coin yields us belongs to money.

Now what does the examination of a coin teach us? It is a shaped piece of metal with a mark upon it. The first point we observe is—(we will speak here of gold, confessedly the best material for coin)—that it is composed of a metal, and that this metal is a very valuable commodity. It is an article very expensive to procure, possessed of high value before it was manufactured into a coin. Whoever has obtained a sovereign, whether on the sale of goods or in payment of a debt, has given twenty shillings worth of property to acquire it. It has cost miners in distant regions, and under circumstances often of great difficulty and trial, a large amount of labour and a heavy expenditure for maintenance and tools, to extract it from the bowels of the earth. They can afford to part with it only on the same general conditions as those on which iron or tin miners give their metals to the community. They must be repaid their expenses and receive an adequate reward for the services which they render to society. The quantity of gold won is small compared with the cost of working a gold mine; gold consequently is dear: a small portion of it will fetch in exchange a large amount of other commodities. This satisfaction must be rendered to the miners or the gold coin will not be produced: and every one who acquires that coin in succession, except as a gift, has been obliged to restore to the person from whom he got it the cost originally paid to the miner. This is a fact of capital importance in currency. No man acquires a piece of metallic currency, of money, except by giving for it its full value in other goods. From this fact it necessarily follows that to sell property and to receive in the place of it golden coins, money, is no increase of riches. It is an exchange of two equal quantities of wealth, of a precious metal for some other article. In the estimation of the two parties to a purchase, the coin is worth the property, and the property the coin; and that is the whole of the matter. The bearing of this truth on the common idea that money is in a peculiar sense riches—that the object of all trade should be to obtain money—that a trade which exports more goods than it imports, and brings in the difference in gold is the truly beneficial trade—that gold is a possession more to be rejoiced in than any other by every nation is obvious and will be considered hereafter.

The question immediately arises: Why do civilized nations buy this costly metal? Property is given away for it at all hours: what has led to such a practice? It is easy to understand the pursuit of food and clothing, of ornaments for house and garden; they are desired for consumption and enjoyment. But it is otherwise with a coin. It is not procured for pleasure or ornamentation—nay, it is obtained to be parted with at the earliest opportunity. It yields nothing whatever to its possessor, except when it leaves him. This energetic desire to acquire money at heavy cost must find its gratification in something which money bestows in the act of going away again. To keep it is wholly without profit or enjoyment; what, then, is the explanation of this incessant purchase of gold and equally incessant parting with it as soon as got? The answer is plain. Coin is manufactured in order to effect a service: in other words, it is a tool, which has the work it performs as the sole reason for its being made. It renders a useful and valuable service. In the act of passing away money is a tool: it does its work, not by staying in its owner's hands, but by leaving them: no other conception of coin is rational or intelligible. It may be purchased long before it is used, as Napoleon I. stored many millions of pounds at the Tuileries in readiness for possible war, or as bankers pile up reserves to guard against the uncertainty of the payment of their debts being suddenly demanded of them. But this changes nothing in the nature of money: it only indicates that it is occasionally wise with money, as with other tools, to provide a stock of it beforehand, lest it may not be procurable at the moment when it is required for use. The truth always remains the same that money is of no utility whatever except when employed as a tool, that is, except when it exercises its proper function by being got rid of in exchange for other property. It is a machine—a means, not an end—an instrument of the same class as a ship or a cart, a means of conveyance. The common cart transfers weights, the money cart transfers ownership. Who ever bought a cart for the purpose of enjoyment in itself? What man, not under a delusion, ever bought money, coin, except with the object of exchanging it for something which he needed?

But why was such a tool required? A cart which should transport weights which human arms could not carry is an obvious want. The intervention of coin at first sight is not so apparent. Yet the need of money in some form is one of the most urgent wants which beset humanity. Without its aid society would be brought to a stand-still, for the very decisive reason that those who wanted to obtain particular goods would otherwise be seldom able to find sellers who would be willing to accept those which they had to offer in exchange.

The tailor might starve before he found a baker who was in want of a coat. This great want is the consequence of the most distinguishing peculiarity of social existence, the division of labour—or rather the separation of employments. This is the fundamental law of society. Whether in a small village or a great nation, whether in a poor land or in a country filled with gigantic manufactures, the same phenomenon ever presents itself; the providing of the multitudinous things which human life consumes is distributed naturally and necessarily amongst special makers. No man above a savage supplies all his own wants; every one has recourse to fellow-men for procuring every article that he uses, except those very few which he can make himself. Here springs up at once the great problem—by what method and upon what principle can he obtain these things made by others? Only by exchanging, by giving to others what he made for them, and receiving from others what they made for him. But for exchanging each party to it must desire to acquire the articles which the other offers, otherwise he will refuse to exchange. This dilemma might arise with every article needed. The hatter might find neither baker nor butcher nor shoemaker who was in want of a hat; direct barter would be impossible, and his trouble might be great. To overcome this difficulty—a difficulty which would have been fatal to civilization—money was invented; and it removes the obstacle perfectly. The action of money is to substitute double for single barter, and the difficulty is instantly conquered by it. The impediment to exchanging was that one of the exchangers did not want the article offered by the other; the solution consisted in interposing a third article, for which each of the two articles might be separately bartered. Go and barter your hat for money, cried the shoemaker, then bring me that money, and the shoes shall be yours. In other words, the shoemaker demands money, and with it he selects for himself in any shop any article that he desires to attain. That is the action and essence of the use of money. A sale for money is thus half a transaction—the exchange is completed only when the shoemaker has obtained with the hatter's money at his own choice one of those commodities which was his motive for engaging in the manufacture of shoes.

1. The first point to be noticed in the transaction is that the seller must feel sure that all other tradesmen will consent to do exactly the same thing that he has done—will give him their goods for money as readily as he gave away his shoes for it. Now this assurance rests only on voluntary consent; no law commands traders to sell for money. A banking oracle of great eminence once expressed unbounded astonishment on being told that a shopkeeper was not bound to give his goods away for money; he confounded the voluntary affixing of money prices on goods with the

obligation imposed by the law of legal tender of discharging debts with money. Aristotle knew better, but then he was a scientific analyst rarely equalled among men. He stated that men "agreed" to take money in exchanging; and it is a matter of voluntary agreement to this hour.

2. But what is the foundation of this voluntary agreement to take money? A seller cannot part with his property in exchange for money which is useless to him unless it furnishes him with a guarantee that in the end he shall procure by its means as much property as he gave away. How does money supply him with such a guarantee? By the value of the metal, as a commodity, in the metal market, of which the money, the coin, is composed. The coin places in the hands of a tailor a portion of metal which is worth to a goldsmith as much as a coat is to the tailor. The one function of the tool of exchange is to give to a seller a guarantee, a thoroughly trustworthy security, that he shall get by a second purchase all that he gave away on the first. This is as truly, as essentially, the work of money as to cut is the work of a knife. This work is performed by giving value for value, and it is precisely because he gets value for value that a seller parts with his property without hesitation. He knows that the same feeling will act on every other trader; with metallic currency, with coin, every one has a complete assurance that he gets in money a commodity worth that which he is selling.

The convenience of having a common tool to serve as a medium of exchange is overwhelming; every shop-keeper will take the coin, because every one in succession is exchanging equal property for property. It is the value of the gold in the metal market which enables the tool of exchange to command equal goods in every shop. Double barter, the hat exchanged for money, and the money in turn exchanged for shoes, thus effects one exchange, a hat for shoes, by the agency of two half-transactions: such is the action of money.

But many deny the accuracy of this analysis. It is the coining, they say, the stamp impressed on the money, which gives it its value. The worth, the buying power of a sovereign, they insist, is settled by the stamp. The Mint coins an ounce of gold into £3, 17s. 10½d. Here is the definition of a pound, and a pound is the meaning and worth of a sovereign. The absurdity of these assertions is so ludicrous that it would scarcely be worth the trouble to refute them, were it not for the obstinate tenacity with which so many persons cling to them, to the consequent confusion of all ideas on currency. If the stamp gave value to the coin, the same stamp on a piece of copper would bestow on it equal value with a golden sovereign, and the decree of the Mint would enable it to buy an equal quantity of goods in the shops—which, in the language of Euclid, "is absurd." If a copper coin could be obtained from the miners only at the same cost with a gold one, they both would be equally valuable; but it cannot, and so the goldsmith will give a vast deal more for the gold coin than the coppersmith will for the copper one; and that is the very reason why every seller will give many more goods for the one than he will for the other. That money is a commodity, and acts by virtue of being a commodity, was clearly perceived by Aristotle. "Men agreed," he remarks, "for exchanging to give and take one of the useful things," that is, a commodity, and consequently a commodity has ever been the instrument of buying, the tool of exchange. In one country furs, in ancient times cattle, sometimes rock-salt; at this day, amongst the Tartars, small cubes of compressed tea, most frequently some metal. Aristotle's dictum is abundantly verified at the present hour, in the case of English money, for sovereigns which foreigners have purchased with their goods are constantly melted down abroad into ingots—a proceeding which could not possibly take place if the stamped sovereign were worth more than the gold it contains. It is the intrinsic value of the metal, its cost as a commodity, which does all the work of a coin.

The absurdity of the notion that the Mint, by coining sovereigns, assigns to them their value, is refuted at once by the remark that when gold was some fifteen times dearer than it is now—that is, when a quantity of other commodities fifteen times larger had to be given to the miner to persuade him to dig the same quantity of gold out of the earth—the same coin purchased fifteen times as many other goods as it would now. Prices were then fifteen times lower in nominal amount. A buyer puts his own value on his money quite as really as the seller does upon his goods. Each party values for himself his own commodity in the act of barter called a purchase. Those who bring in the Mint as a regulator of price have no conception of the answer to be made to Sir Robert Peel's famous question, "What is a pound?" The answer, no doubt, is furnished by the Mint, not in value, but in quantity. The Mint replies by setting an arithmetical sum. Given that 20 shillings make a pound and 12 pence a shilling, it declares that a pound is that part of an ounce of gold which will produce £3, 17s. 10½d. for the whole ounce; in other words, it proclaims that in law and fact a pound is so many carats weight of gold. These carats are contained in the current coin called a sovereign; so that a pound is another name for a sovereign. Whenever a pound comes before a court of law, it will compel a sovereign to be given for a pound. Not a trace of value is contained in the expression.

3. The Mint imposes a stamp on the coin; for what purpose? To give information; to make known, on the word of the Government, that the coined sovereign handled is made of standard gold and possesses in full the prescribed weight. In the words, again, of Aristotle, "impressing a stamp on the money, to relieve men of

the trouble of measuring it." As Mr Adams has well phrased it, "to save every man the trouble of carrying about with him a bottle of acid and a pair of scales." Ingots have to be tested before they are received in payment; a stamped sovereign or dollar tells every one what it is. Nothing can be more obvious than this fact; yet how many, even intelligent men, have been puzzled to say what the stamp it bears does for a sovereign.

4. Although any commodity, in principle, may serve as the tool of exchange, practically, every nation that could obtain the precious metals has employed them as money. They had excellent reasons for the choice. Gold and silver are very portable, that is, they are light compared with their great value, clean to handle, beautiful to look at, go into small compass, hard and therefore enduring in use, retain the marking stamp easily and long, and extremely divisible. They bear being cut into coins of different size, with proportionate value to their weights. When much worn, they still possess a perfectly real value up to what remains of metal in the coins. The bullocks of Diomed and America must have been very awkward money, most hard to dispose of till the time came for making purchases with them; they required stables and food. The precious metals do not deteriorate in their physical qualities by being handled and used. Cattle-money is very perishable; equally so lumps of rock-salt. Nor can cattle be divided; an ox could be dealt

with only as a whole; a piece could not be cut off from him to serve as small change. Then again coins, especially gold ones, if no longer wanted for money, are readily convertible into pure metals, retaining their full value as commodities for use. The demonetisation of gold would not injure holders of full weighted sovereigns or dollars; they would be converted into jewels and ornaments at once. Lastly, the precious metals possess in an eminent degree the first requisite of good money, steadiness of value. The essence of the action of money lies in the guarantee it gives for purchasing other goods of equal value with those given for it; a changeable guarantee breaks down in its most vital quality. Every contract, every debt, supposes that the value understood at the time shall be paid when due. Absolute certainty on this point is not obtainable; because value is expressed in a commodity, and there is not a single commodity which is not liable to some fluctuation of value. But the money which is made of the steadiest commodity is incomparably the best. Professor Sumner humorously points out the unsoundness of the guarantee furnished by several forms of money, or rather of the tool of exchange. "If a cow will pay taxes, as it did in America, the leanest cow will be given. If corn will pay a debt, the corn which is of poorest quality, or is damaged, will be paid." No doubt, gold and silver, on the discovery of America, sustained a heavy change of permanent value, to the great disturbance of all contracts and debts stipulating payment in these metals. They may subsequently have undergone some further depreciation, although this by no means must be taken as proved; nevertheless they are less open to the charge of changeableness than any other commodities.

These weighty considerations combined have prevailed in establishing metallic coin as the universal money; and this money is a collection of small portions of a precious metal, called coins, whose weight and purity are attested by the State.

The right of attesting the public money, of coining, is usually claimed as a prerogative inherent in the State; but this doctrine belongs to a political philosophy which is fast passing away. Thomas Aquinas saw the truth long before it dawned on the mass of mankind—"*Rex datur propter regnum, non regnum propter regem.*" Whatever authority or right is possessed by rulers had its origin in the interest of the whole people; but mediæval kings, who reaped large profits from the adulteration of the coin, were slow to perceive the application of this principle to currency. That coining should be exclusively vested in the State rests on a vastly stronger foundation than prerogative; the State can do the work best, and that reason is sufficient and decisive. That the public money should be honest and be what it professes to be, deeply concerns the public welfare; and no attestation furnished by private persons can compete in authority with the stamp imposed by the Government Mint. Private persons are capable of putting as good coin into circulation as the State, just as they circulate ingots; still no authentication can give a warranty as good as that of the State.

5. Our analysis lastly teaches us the origin of the expression Currency. It is derived from the Latin *curro*, I run; and our description shows that money runs. It circulates. Its office is to place certain goods in a buyer's hands: that done, it leaves him in order to repeat the same operation for the seller who took it. He has no motive—save occasionally for a spare stock —for keeping the money; he accepted it for his goods only to buy with it in turn. The sooner he calls upon it to fulfil its office, and to run away from him, and to transfer itself to the pocket of some other seller, the better. The faster money circulates, the greater is the quantity of work got out of it. The longer it lies in a pocket or a till, the more it assumes the character of a cart or a plough lying unused under a shed.

We now reach the second great benefit conferred by money. It was invented in order to escape the insuperable difficulty presented by single barter to the exchanging of the products of industry, which, by the law of human life, no man can make entirely for himself. So they are all first bartered for money, and the money re-exchanged for other goods. Thus, as a necessary consequence, every commodity is compared with money;

the quantity of money to be given for a particular quantity of the article is determined; in other words, every article acquires its price. But, by the fact that each article is compared with money, and its exchangeable value with money affirmed, all commodities can be compared in value with one another. Price is the value of an article calculated in money; and as every article has its price, the prices of all can be compared with another. Money becomes a standard of measurement, precisely as the yard is the standard of length. Lengths and distances can be stated as longer or shorter than each other by each being expressed in yards; so the relative worth of saleable goods is measured by the worth of each singly being expressed in money. Thus money is the common measure of value. Money, however, I conceive, was not invented for effecting this great service of providing a common measure of value; the service was the result of the fact that money, by its very nature, was measured in barter against every commodity, all being sold for money. To get over the difficulty that a seller of goods might not want the other goods offered by the buyer was alone the true origin of money.

It is very important to bear in mind that money does not determine value; money only expresses it. Value is determined by each man's personal feeling. The maker or owner, on the one side—and the motives which act on his feeling may be most numerous and varied—decides how much he must receive in exchange before he consents to part with his property. When he proceeds to sell, he meets a counter feeling, a counter estimation of the values of the property and the money in the buyer. The resultant between these two forces is the market value of the commodity at the time. In the exchange, the gold and the commodity are valued on identically the same conditions; the money is as much bought as the coat which it purchases.

The equality of position of the buyer and the seller leads up to the question—What is the value, the market price, of gold? How is it to be expressed? Put in this form, the question admits of no single answer. The market value or price of a sovereign is a hat for the hatter, a pair of shoes for the shoemaker, and so on throughout all the list of things sold. A hat is the price of a sovereign, just as a sovereign is the price of a hat. But the answer we are in seach of will be found in the analysis of what is implied in an act of barter. What is the value of a coat to a tailor? Its cost of production, including the reward—both in wages and profit—without which he will not make the coat? It is the same with the gold of money—either the owner of it or the miner from whom he ultimately got it calculates its value in the same identical manner. If the miner fails to obtain for his gold ore a quantity of goods sufficient to replace what the mining has cost him, with a reasonable profit for himself, he gives up the business and abandons the mine. Less gold is produced and the demand for it continues; it rises in value; it exchanges, in buying, for a larger quantity of all other commodities. That is, the price of everything sold falls. On the contrary, a rise in general prices indicates that gold has become cheaper, a larger quantity of it must be given for the same goods.

There remains a question of supreme importance for a clear understanding of currency: the power of dealing with theories of currency, and language used on every side is intimately connected with the question and its answer. How much gold, how many sovereigns or dollars, does a country want? To the multitude the question seems absurd. How can there be too much money? the more money a nation has the better. With money one can buy every thing: money is true riches, so says the mercantile theory, so do English newspapers every day, so say the inflationists of the United States all over that great country. Every arrival of gold from California or Australia is hailed with delight in England; manifestly the country is so much the richer, the money market so much the stronger. But those who talk in this manner totally forget that gold has to be paid for like every thing else. It is a very expensive affair to get gold out of a mine; the glorious ingots which have reached London have not made England one pound the richer. They have all been paid for with English property of equal value. Why then all this rejoicing? There are few more melancholy delusions than this indestructible folly of believing that it is always good for a country to get more money. If farmers were to hail with incessant delight cargoes of carts ever streaming in, men would pity them as insane; yet in what respect are these jubilations over gold more rational? Carts and money are both tools —instruments of conveyance, endowed with the same nature, and subject to the same general laws. The question for each is the same—how many are wanted for the work which they were invented to do? In the case of money, how much gold can a nation use? How much can it find employment for? The answer, as with carts, must be sought from the special work money has to perform—that is, from the amount of exchanging which calls for the agency of this tool, the quantity of property of which the ownership has to be transferred by this instrument. A cart transfers weight; money, ownership; and all the world knows that the cartage to be done determines the number of carts. In the same way, the ownership of property which requires to be transferred by the actual employment of money itself determines how much money there ought to be in a nation. No other answer is possible, unless it is denied that money is only a tool; if so, another explanation of the nature of money must be produced. A certain amount of buying and selling and paying of debts goes on daily in every country through the agency of money; enough for effecting this purpose is wanted and no more. The number of tools needed depends on the quantity of work to be done by them ; that rule comes from the nature itself of a tool, and it is complete. Spare money is desirable, no doubt, just as spare hats and spare shoes, to guard against the inconvenience of there being none when work or accident calls for them ; but this fact does not come into consideration in this place. And further, the necessary quantity of reserve for banks must be reckoned as money needed for use. The one point is, has every man who wants to buy or pay with coin a coin to do it with ? If he has, the supply of money is complete ; all further purchase of coin or money is senseless and a waste.

But an important distinction must be noticed here. The same collective amount of cash transactions will not always require the same quantity of money. The same coin may effect few or many purchases, according to the circumstances of the locality. In a gambling house the same dollar or sovereign may settle twenty transactions in a quarter of an hour. In the great West it may remain weeks or months in a farmer's pocket before it can be used. In a nation in which life moves slowly, or buyers or sellers live wide asunder, or when no credit is given, a much larger number of coins will be required to settle transactions which could be completed by much fewer but more rapidly moving coins under the opposite circumstances. Hence rapidity of circulation when practicable will diminish the quantity of money or coins required. The rule, however, remains the same under either circumstances; enough money to carry out the cash business, be it much or little, must be provided, and no more; for more cannot be used (omitting spare stocks), all merchants, shop-keepers, inflationists, bankers, stock exchanges, and newspapers notwithstanding. We thus make a deduction of considerable scientific value, that the question of the distribution of the precious metals, on which so much stress is so often laid, is at bottom only a question of the commercial habits of different countries and localities. A nation is not the poorer for having little gold, nor the richer for having much, if only it has enough. The precious metals flow to countries of low civilisation, of political insecurity, where the law is weak and justice uncertain; also to nations using large banking reserves, of which more hereafter; whilst they find scant resting-place in lands of high commercial development, where property is safe, credit secure, the recovery of debts easy and to be relied upon, and where the owners of goods are willing to part with them for cheques and bills, and similar processes of deferred payment. There is probably no country in the world which, in comparison with the extent of its wealth and its trade, needs and uses so little money, metallic money, as England.

The inquiry, how is one to discover how much buying and selling and paying of debts is going on in England, so as to learn how many sovereigns are needed, is answered in the same way as the parallel question, how many hats does England require. By practical trial; in no other manner. The rule is, so many heads so many hats; the actual number is discovered experimentally by the hatters. In precisely the same manner is the number of purchases and payments effected by handling sovereigns and dollars ascertained; and just as the hatter ceases to make more hats when every head has got one, so when there is more gold in a country than is wanted for actual work, it first finds its way into the vaults of the bullion dealers or of the Bank of England, and then gradually flies away abroad. If the world were full of gold—that is, if all the requirements for use in payments (its employment in the arts is here omitted) were satisfied, then one of two results must follow; either the miners must diminish producing, or gold must fall in value. It must follow the law of all commodities in excess of demand: it must fall in price, which for gold means, it must be able to buy fewer goods.

But what if a country labours under a deficiency of coin? Is not this a very serious matter, something like a calamity? Nothing of the kind. In the first place it is not a loss of wealth—the country is none the poorer for it; for gold cannot be procured without giving away other property in exchange for it. There would be no diminution of the power to buy goods in the shops and stores because there happened to be less coin, less money, as is so commonly imagined, most of all in America. Goods are bought with other goods; and the country would possess those which must have been sent away to purchase a mere machine for exchanging. And secondly, some inconvenience would arise from a deficiency of a particular tool. But that inconvenience in the case of coin would be something very different in kind from that which would arise if there were too few ploughs or if factory engines were suddenly diminished. In these cases there would necessarily be a diminution of wealth produced; the country would really be the poorer. With coin, there would simply be an impediment to exchanging, that would be all. But there would be no want of means to meet the temporary difficulty. In these modern days a fresh supply would speedily be acquired from foreign countries; gold would be bought abroad, as it must have been had there been no deficiency; and even without that remedy other resources would be at hand. The circulation of the currency would undoubtedly become more rapid, it would run faster and do more work. In a country where banking was largely used, the momentary difficulty would be trifling. (I am not speaking here of a deficiency of banking reserves, that will be considered under banking.) Small cheques would be given in payment till an increased supply of gold had come in. Fifty years ago it was not an uncommon occurrence in England for employers of labour to be short at times of silver, and they were obliged to pay small premiums to get a bag of silver against Saturday evening; but such events have ceased to happen. A run on banks for gold would be a different matter. It does not imply the fact that we are here supposing, a positive deficiency of the money required for ready-money payments in coin all over the country.

One peculiarity of metallic currency deserves notice. Barring existing contracts for fixed payments of coin, agreed to in the past, the public has no interest in the cheapening of gold for currency purposes, as of all other articles. Cheaper tea is an increase of wealth; cheaper gold coin is not. The reason of the difference consists in the fact that the quality by which gold does its work as a tool is value. The same value must be made up with coin; two sovereigns of ten shillings each would be wanted to make a purchase formerly effected with one at twenty. Cheapness or dearness of the precious metal acts only on the weight and size of the coins carrying the same value in the purchase of other commodities—indeed, a great cheapness of gold would create a very serious inconvenience. A golden shilling worth no more than one of silver would be a fearful aggravation of weight; the inevitable result in practice would be an immense disuse of coin, and a proportionate increase of small cheques, small bank-notes, and other machinery for exchanging.

From the fact that a large increase in the production

of gold after the whole world had acquired a full supply for its currency wants would necessarily lead to a fall in its value the inference has been drawn that a similar effect takes place in a single nation, and consequently great importance has been attached to the amount of its circulation. A diminution of gold in England, it has been argued, makes coin dear, and causes a local fall of general prices. An over abundant circulation, it has been held, generates the opposite result, and consequently the amount of the circulation in England is carefully recorded every week. I regard this as a very decided error, and this circulation theory built upon it as an entire mistake. It forgets that the metal of coin, gold, is very portable, easily removable from one country to another. Long before the coin was so scarce as to act on prices, the inconvenience felt would have fetched supplies from abroad very speedily with the modern means of locomotion. The slightest difference in the purchasing powers of gold in two neighbouring lands would swiftly lead to equalisation by importation. The value of gold is the same in all countries within anything like moderate distances. Excess of gold does not lower its value in a single nation, but generates accumulation in banks; it does not remain out in circulation, acting on general prices, like inconvertible notes. At this day sixty millions sterling lie buried in the Bank of France; what possible influence can that hoard or any other hoard exercise on prices? When notes and banking are at work, the quantity of transactions effected by coin then becomes insignificant. In London alone the Clearing House accomplishes more buying and selling in one week than the whole quantity of gold coin in the kingdom amounts to. It follows that the quantity of the so-called circulation of the gold and notes together is quite unimportant; it has no action on prices; it is a curious piece of statistics, and nothing more. All lands are linked together by the steamboat and the railway. The export and import of gold has no significance—unless it be for banking, of which more hereafter. Whether the gold of Australia and California tarries in England, or passes on to pay for French wines or German wools, or American cotton, matters nothing as an occurrence of currency, nay, it may be a great gain. If a bad season has destroyed the harvest, lucky is the country which chances to have a store of gold which it can at once send abroad to buy food. The exportation of the metal causes no diminution of wealth. It was lying idle in a cellar, it departs and brings in capital, food for workmen engaged in the production of wealth. It must not be spoken of as a calamity; it is a thing to rejoice over.

Gold exercises a most valuable function in liquidating the balances of international trade. All trade, as between individuals so between nations, is an exchange of property, of wealth, of goods. Every nation buys abroad with its own products, its own goods—it has nothing else to obtain its purchases with. When a country has mines of gold, gold passes as a product, just as cotton or wine. If the buying equalled the selling every day—as would happen with direct barter—the accounts would always be balanced of themselves. But as purchases and sales with one single foreign country are not always equal, there remains on a given day a balance to settle, and that is done with an export of gold from the country which bought most to the country which has sold most. At times this difference is large, as when a bad harvest or famine urges on immediate and large purchases of food, and sufficient gold at the moment might be difficult to procure. But the machinery of modern commerce here comes in aid; bills—which are only deferred payments—are brought into play, and often, before they are due, the balance has been corrected with the export of goods. In any case, as Adam Smith has well remarked, England can replenish itself with gold from abroad, if she has the wherewithal to pay for it. Trade never is anything else at last but exchange of goods.

International payments require the currencies of different countries to be compared with one another. Each country sells upon prices estimated in its own money; hence in international exchanging two accounts have to be settled together, each expressed in different monies. How is the position of each towards the other to be calculated? They must be reduced to a common measure—to gold. French Napoleons and francs must be converted into weights of gold; so must the English pounds and shillings. This operation is carried out by expressing the coin of the one country in the coin of the other. The weight of gold in an English sovereign is compared with the weight of the same metal in French francs, calculated on the basis of the weight of gold in the twenty-franc piece, the Napoleon. The discovery is made that twenty-five francs, and some $\frac{11}{100}$ths more, express the same weight of gold as the English sovereign, and this equality is called the par of exchange. When the exchange is at par, a man who has an English sovereign can obtain these francs, and *vice versa* the francs will get a sovereign. A bullion dealer who bought two heaps of sovereigns and Napoleons on this basis, and melted the gold into ingots, would get exactly the same quantity of ingots from each heap.

But exchange seldom stands at par between two countries, for a very sufficient reason: the buying and selling is seldom equal on the same day; the difference, as explained, they agree shall be liquidated in gold. Now to send gold involves a charge for carriage and insurance; and the man who has to send it will avoid this charge if he can. Goods purchased in foreign countries, all except the small balance liquidated in gold, are paid by the exchange of debts, by bills. The English debtor pays his French creditor by sending him a bill due by a French debtor for English goods sent to France. If the purchases in the two countries are equal, so will be the bills created by them. If not, then some debtor will be unable to find a bill, and every debtor in the country which has to pay most to the other will compete with all the others not to be the man who will have to incur the expense of sending gold. He will offer for a bill rather more than its value in metal at the par of exchange. The Frenchman will give at Paris say 25¼ francs for a pound due in London rather than send gold. If trade had moved in the opposite direction, and England owed more to France than France to England, it will be the English debtor in London who will be eager to buy in London a bill due by a Frenchman in France; he will give a sovereign for 24¾ francs to be paid in France. In the former case the exchange is said to be in favour of England; the Englishman gets a quarter of a franc more than the gold of his pound at par. In the second case, the exchange is pronounced unfavourable; the Englishman gets less gold in 24¾ francs than he gave away in his pound. A favourable exchange implies that England has sold more than she has bought; she has a balance to receive in gold. An unfavourable exchange implies the reverse, that is, she is a debtor on that day's settlement. But the exchange will not rise above par beyond the cost of carriage and insurance for the transmission of gold. If it costs half-a-franc to send a pound's weight of gold to England, the Parisian debtor will accept an exchange which makes him give 25½ francs for a pound to be paid in England, but he will refuse one of 25¾; it will cost him less to send the gold.

Falser and more misleading expressions cannot be conceived than the terms favourable and unfavourable exchanges. They survive still the memorable refutation of their untruth by Adam Smith; they involve ignorance of the very nature of all trade; they efface the living fact that men buy of foreign countries to procure goods for use and consumption, that all trade is only an exchange of goods. This language is profoundly unconscious that gold is a mere tool. It teaches that gold, or coin, or money, is an end, a good thing for its own sake, an article worth giving one's wealth to obtain. It is saturated with the Mercantile Theory, so utterly in vain has Adam Smith written. These words express satisfaction at the proof that England has sold more than she has bought, spreading the delusion that an excess of exports over imports is an excellent state of trade; that it is a good thing to spend and consume wealth in making iron and yarns, and to get gold in the place of them,—for what object they do not say. They perpetuate the merchant's and the shopkeeper's absurdity that to sell is everything, ignorant that to sell without buying is to convert a man into a Midas, and to make him perish amidst piles of gold. The value set on favourable exchanges is the greatest intellectual and literary wonder of our age.

It remains to say a few words on a double standard. In some countries a gold or a silver coin is a legal tender for the payment of debts. The expression legal tender arises only on the payment of a contract to pay money, of a debt; it means that the law will declare the debt to have been paid, if the legal tender, money, has been given. A double standard gives the debtor the choice of paying in gold or silver coin as he pleases. Now if the value of the metal given in the metal market is the same, whether gold or silver has been offered, the contract is justly fulfilled, and neither party has an advantage over the other. The law fixes the relative quantities of the two coins or metals which may be given. In England it says that twenty shillings and one sovereign are the same money. But unfortunately the law cannot secure that the metallic value of either silver or gold will remain unchanged; if there is an alteration in the value of either, it is plain that twenty shillings may be worth more or less than a sovereign. A debtor will always choose to pay in the coin which is cheapest, which it costs him less of his wealth to obtain. If silver becomes cheaper than gold, the English gold sovereign will be sold abroad to buy silver, which will be brought to the English Mint to be coined, and debts will be paid with it with a profit. Hence the practical rule has been laid down that the inferior currency will expel all others from a country, that is, the money whose metal is valued too highly in the coin in the proportions established between the coin of both metals will be sought by all debtors, because they can purchase it with a profit with the metal which is introduced in the coin. In England the proportion of twenty shillings to the pound has long existed, in spite of many fluctuations in the metallic value of silver. The banishment of the gold has been prevented by the declaration that silver shall not be a legal tender beyond forty shillings. This has kept shillings a purely subsidiary money —over-valued, with too little silver in them to be a twentieth part of a golden sovereign, but not so little, and they not so numerous, as to make it worth while for coiners to manufacture them out of honest silver. A double standard seems to me unsupported by adequate reasons, and it entails the injustice that a debtor is enabled by it to pay his creditor with a smaller value of metal than was contracted for.*

* See Appendix A, page 173.

CHAPTER II.

PAPER CURRENCY.

Section I.—Convertible Bank-Notes.

WE have now ascertained the nature and principles of a metallic currency; we proceed to paper currency, and we shall find the same general principles to prevail here also, subject only to such modifications of detail as are created by the difference between paper and metal. Coin and bank-notes perform generally the same work. They transfer property, and thus exchange commodities. Both were invented to effect the same purpose. What we have gained in the study of metallic currency must be firmly adhered to, or mischievous untruth will be the result.

But it is necessary to explain the word currency. In America the expression is frequently used to denote instruments of exchange other than money—all those, namely, that consist of paper; but this is a practice much to be deprecated. There is too much confusion already in currency to excuse the increase of it by affixing new senses to old words. This mode of speaking is further open to the objection that it classes under one term things very dissimilar; for a cheque and a bank-note are very different matters. A cheque is not currency, does not run. The word currency is needed as a generic term to comprise two varieties of similar tools which are current and circulate, and are universally called money. Both stay out in the hands of the public. A cheque, on the contrary, travels straightway to the bank which has to pay it. A bill is slightly more current; it may pass, as a tool of exchange, through a few hands by the help of endorsements, but it has a fixed day for being paid and annihilated. There is one distinction more between these machines for payment and the bank-note. They are personal, so to speak. Every man who takes them knows that he is bound, for his own safety, to weigh their signatures. There is a distinct act of reflection in giving goods for cheques or bills. Hence, in popular language, they are not money, things which everybody takes as a matter of course. The bank-note, on the contrary, is almost impersonal. It is, in a manner, semi-anonymous; when a bank is once thoroughly established, its notes travel unchallenged all over the town.

But is the bank-note, for all that, money? It is called money; so are bills, occasionally. Cheques earn the title still more frequently. A shopkeeper, when he carries bills, cheques, and cash, to the bank, calls them all money. Even Mr Bagehot, in his

"Lombard Street," written expressly to explain the Money Market as being "as concrete and real as anything else, capable of being described in as plain words, so that it is the writer's fault if what he says is not clear," gives six different meanings to the word money. What, after this in a writer of ability and reputation, must be the state of mind of ordinary mortals upon apparently so well known a thing as money? And this marvellous looseness of expression runs the same course in private as in commercial life. A rich man is said to have so much money in cash or in railway stock. The objects comprehended under this multiple word by popular language are as countless as the sand on the sea-shore.

Coin, metallic coin, alone is true money, and nothing else is, unless it be a commodity, as an ox, or a cow, or a piece of salt. There is a very decisive reason for this assertion. Every kind of paper styled money carries on its face an order or promise to pay money; and without that order or promise it would be a worthless piece of paper and nothing more. An order or promise to give a thing is not the thing itself; the thing is absent. This settles the matter absolutely: paper is not money. It is idle to reply that the distinction is unimportant—that the bank-note does the same work as money, and that practically there is no harm in calling it money. I answer that the harm is immense for the understanding of currency. The vital fact is obscured that the man who takes a gold coin for his goods receives an actual piece of property, a metal, as valuable as the thing he sells. He acquires not a particle of substance with a cheque or a bank-note. If the cheque is dishonoured or the bank breaks, he finds a nothing in his hand against the wealth that he gave away. If cheques and bank-notes are true money, then so are spoken words, for they can purchase property, and bind the buyer at law just as strongly as a cheque. To tell a bookseller to put five pounds' worth of books to his account commits the buyer to payment as completely as a cheque. Coin is the substance, the reality covenanted to be given for goods bought; consequently coin alone is payment. The coin at last may never be touched, because it may be put down in an account against which set-offs appear on the debtor and creditor sides; coin then is not asked for, because its equivalent in property has been received. Everything else—spoken words, shop-accounts, bank-notes, cheques, warrants—are nothing but title-deeds, evidence good at law to compel the stipulated payments in coin, if not voluntarily given. Without a court of law in the background, they are only acknowledgments resting on honour, and may at any moment prove to be empty writing. Coin pays, no form of paper does till what is written upon it is fulfilled. A bank-note is not property placed in a man's hands; every seller may decline to take it. If the bank fails, the holder will never be paid at all.

The truth that bank-notes are not money received

a remarkable confirmation from an elaborate judgment delivered in the Supreme Court of the United States. The question which presented itself for final decision was whether debts which had been contracted previously to the Act of Congress, which made the inconvertible bank-notes called greenbacks legal tender, were discharged by the tender of these notes. Nothing could be sounder or more admirable than the doctrine laid down by Chief Justice Chase. He ruled that such debts were contracts to deliver money, and that bank-notes were not money, and could not be forced upon a creditor as a satisfaction of his claim. The distinction that coin alone, the metallic dollar, was money, was most sharply and accurately drawn, and the right of the creditor to the covenanted payment as clearly established. A bank-note was pronounced not to be payment; it did not fulfil the contract entered into to deliver money. The case was wholly different with debts contracted subsequently to the enactment of the law which declared greenbacks legal tender. The creditor had been distinctly warned beforehand that the word dollar would be understood by the law to mean that particular piece of paper which contained an acknowledgement of debt due by the Government of the United States. He knew when he gave credit on an undertaking to be repaid in dollars that he would receive, not money, but the transfer of a debt expressed on paper which was due by the Government. He did not stipulate for money, and consequently money he was not entitled to and would not receive. He would get dollars, as interpreted by the law of legal tender, not the metallic dollars which are money, but a promise made by the Government to pay such dollars, without any stipulation as to the time when they would be given. It was for him to consider when he gave away his goods, what the promise of a dollar or the piece of paper might be worth in the stores.

Nevertheless, though bank-notes are not money, it is hopeless to try to strip them of that title. When the bank-notes are established in public confidence, it is impossible to maintain the distinction between them and coin in popular language. Mixed together in the same purse, the common heap is regarded as money. They both do the same work, both circulate and purchase with equal ease, both raise no other idea than that they are money to buy with. The radical distinction, however, between them, that coin makes a real payment and notes do not, is of the utmost scientific importance; the difference meets the inquirer at every turn in examining the nature and action of bank-notes.

But it is otherwise with the applications of the word money referred to above. Every man who has the interest of Political Economy at heart, and wishes to guard against the mischievous consequences of an unsound currency, is bound to protest against such an abuse of language. The abbreviations and the slang of the Stock Exchange and of banking incessantly corrupt ideas on currency; confusion of language ever begets confusion of thought.

Let us now examine how it comes to pass that a bank-note is able to act as money. Coin places in the hands of a seller a commodity as valuable as his own. The value of the metal of the coin in the metal market furnishes him with a trustworthy guarantee that he will be able with it to buy in any shop another commodity worth as much as the one he sold. A guarantee is the essence of a tool of exchange: what is the guarantee supplied by a bank-note? The answer rests on a practical fact. Experience shows that men are willing to sell on credit—that is, on deferred payment; for that is the meaning of credit. They rely on the law which compels debtors to make payment at the due time; if there is no law they can rely upon, as in barbarous countries, they will not sell on credit. Credit next takes a further step as civilisation expands; a seller will give away his goods not only on the credit of the buyer, he will also be willing to accept a debt due to him as payment. This is the essence of the action of a bank-note. Such a note acknowledges that the issuer owes the money stamped on it to the holder of the note. A seller by taking the bank-note makes himself the creditor of the Government or bank, and is willing to part with his property, substantially, on credit to the State or bank. He finds in this debt, now due to him, of the issuer of the bank-note a sufficient guarantee for being able to buy with it other goods. Such a guarantee suffices also for the seller all over the town. The guarantee of a coin is value, not physical qualities; a good debt is regarded universally as possessing equal value; hence it does as well as the coin. Every buyer with a note virtually says:—"I have no money; give me the goods and I will tell a good man who owes me money to pay you for me." That is the action of a bank-note and cheque. This is satisfactory to the seller. He does not want the coin as coin, but as value, and a sound debt is as valuable. The paper money has some special advantages; it is light to carry and far easier to keep in safety than coin, whilst, by the help of the number marked upon it, it imparts considerable security against robbery.

Thus a bank-note is an excellent tool of exchange, but on one vital condition, that it is as trustworthy as the metal itself of the coin. The instant that the note is unable to procure the gold mentioned on its face, because the debtor is supposed to be insolvent, it sinks into a mere piece of paper. Its holder is now unable to buy with it: he must keep it as a bad debt, for whatever it may prove to yield ultimately.

Paper money has one further superiority of great importance over coin: its comparative cheapness combined with equal efficiency. Twenty shillings' worth of English wealth must have been given to a foreign miner to procure a sovereign; a bank-note costs less than sixpence. This gain to England, this saving on the cost of the indispensable tool of exchange, extends to every bank-note in circulation; how vast the capital is thus rescued and kept for the maintenance of English industry, whilst the supply of the fitting tools is complete, is obvious.

We come now to the very important and much-debated inquiry, how these paper machines for exchanging ought to come into existence. The cheque and the bill possess an individual character; they are created and ended by single transactions; particular goods are purchased with them; the banker pays the cheque, the acceptor the bill, and both cheque and bill disappear. The origin of the bank-note is not so obvious. Assuming, for the present, that it has been issued by a bank, how did the bank manage to get it into circulation? By paying its debts with it. A bank owes money to its depositors; when they draw it out, they are generally willing, nay prefer, to receive it in the form of bank-notes. It is the same when a Government is the issuer. It owes money—whether to pay interest on a national debt, or on the purchase of supplies and stores for its wants; it pays with notes, which pledge the actual giving of coin at some future time. A Government, however, when it becomes an issuer of notes, invariably enacts a law making them legal tender, whereas banks do not obtain and do not require this privilege to enable their notes to circulate. The reason of the difference is clear. A bank can be compelled by a note-holder to give the money stipulated on pain of bankruptcy; the assurance that a Government will always pay is by no means so certain. There are no means for compelling a Government to pay money, if it chooses to say that it has none, and it would find great difficulty, from the knowledge of this fact, in persuading contractors to take its notes in payment. So it has recourse for help to this privilege of legal tender conferred by law on its notes. A contractor who is assured that his own creditors must take these notes in payment becomes willing to give his goods to the Government in exchange for them; he can pass them on to others, and that is everything.

But there is a very solid and serious distinction between a private issuer of notes and a Government. The property given to a solvent banker for his notes is not lost to the nation; the banker lends it, if he is a good banker, to persons who do not waste or destroy it, but employ it as capital. The public pays exactly the same for the tool of exchange, whether it procures it from a miner or from a bank. But when the wealth is given to a miner, he consumes it; the nation retains, no doubt, an equal value of gold, but it is lost as capital beyond the work of exchanging in buying and paying. Its services as a tool are all that the nation gets from it. The same services are procured from the bank-note, only it costs but sixpence to the banker and to the nation. Compared with a £5 note, wealth to the extent of £4, 19s 6d, which must have been sent away to a foreign miner, now remains in England, and if the banker does not mismanage his business, is set to work as a part of the wealth-producing capital of the nation. But Government issues are directly united with consumption; the Government spends and consumes what it procures with its notes; it is not employed as capital. No Government which acquired the whole paper circulation of a country could be trusted for not consuming what it procured with it, whereas in England every pound of the Bank of England issues, except what the law commands to be kept in gold as reserve, is capital at work in the creation of wealth. This capital is given to the Bank by the holders of its bank-notes, and the Bank places it in the hands of men who employ it and reproduce it in goods made.

To stand on a level with coin as a tool of exchange or currency, the debt expressed by the banker must be as valuable as the coin. With metallic money the public possesses certain knowledge—it holds the precious metal in its hands. How is it to feel equally assured as to paper money? How is it to acquire a well-warranted confidence that the debt remains good, that the issuing banker can always pay for it, because he is as perfectly solvent? By convertibility, that is, not only by the right to demand coin for the note at any moment, but also by the fact itself that the coin demanded is actually given. How, then, is convertibility to be secured? This leads to the farther question, who ought to be the issuers of the paper circulation of a country—the Government or a bank or banks?

With regard to the respective fitnesses of each of these two issuers for the function, very diverse opinions are maintained. On the side of the bankers, it is urged that the bank-note—as its name indicates—is historically the offspring of banks. In substance it is the same as the cheque, an order on or an undertaking by a bank to pay a sum of money. Further, it is an ordinary commercial transaction, and has existed as such in many countries, and the State is not warranted in invading the domain of private life. The note circulation of Scotland is appealed to as a proof of the excellence which private issues may attain to, bank-notes being actually preferred to sovereigns by the Scotch—and where is a more acute and intelligent population to be found than the Scotch?

The advocates of the issue by Government take their stand on prerogative. The function, they urge, is essentially a public act—it covers the whole nation. The profit derived from so national an operation ought fitly to be reaped by the public. Omitting existing issuers, no injury is done to a particular individual by appropriating the issues to the State. The Parliament of England, they point out, acted on this principle in

1844; it laid the foundation of the ultimate extinction of private issues, and erected a Government office as the sold distributor of bank-notes in the future.

It seems to me that if the issuing of notes were commenced for the first time it would be difficult to resist the argument that the profits of a function which embraces the whole people naturally belongs to the people itself. Bank issues are local. A currency comprehending the whole community is of a higher order, so that even if the agency of banks were called for, some portion of the profits might justly be reserved for the State. The bank's right to have its cheques undisturbed is indisputable—they are personal relations of individuals to it. The solution of the question, however, will in almost all cases be determined by the circumstances of the day and place; local arguments may at any time turn the scale in favour of either party. In England private banks had proved themselves to be bad and unsafe issuers of public currency. The Act of 1844 wisely and justly substituted for them issues controlled by the State. In Scotland the private issues have displayed on trial unchallengeable quality; few persons, not doctrinaires, would dream of suppressing them in favour of Government notes, except under some call of necessity. In America there is entire liberty of action. Government and banks issue together. Hence when a final arrangement is made for rendering all the notes convertible, some principle must be found and carried out. It is a matter of great gravity.

Direct issue by a Government appears to me to be an objectionable machinery for the management of a paper currency. It fails on the capital point of providing thoroughly trustworthy security for convertibility. A Government cannot be declared legally insolvent. A President of the United States or a Prime Minister of England cannot be locked up in prison if multitudes of their fellow-countrymen are reduced to ruin by the bankruptcy of the State. "No more gold in the till," would be an answer to the presenter of a note which would place the Bank of England in the Insolvency Court; what harm would it do to a single Government official employed in managing the paper currency? Hence responsibility for maintaining convertibility cannot be fastened on political rulers as it can on a private company. They are not liable in person or in purse. They can always plead for refusing to pay gold, "The State acknowledges the debt, and you will be paid at last, but you must wait a while now." But what does this mean? That the national currency is instantly corrupted, that all kinds of value will soon be put upon the bank-notes, that the essential function of currency to furnish a guarantee to the man who receives it—that he will be able to buy as valuable goods with it as those he sold—will be lost, that every one will be in perplexity as to the worth of the paper money which he puts down in his account-book when he sells on credit, and then the whole trade of the country becomes poisoned with uncertainty and disorder. Politicians, and indeed tax-payers also, are not to be trusted for being proof against the temptation of being indifferent about a deterioration of the currency, if only it helps them in an hour of difficulty. A purely metallic currency would furnish them with no resource; but to get property with paper is easy and pleasant for a Government, and they can always plead necessity at pleasure. The conclusion is that a Government is a bad direct issuer of paper currency, and every nation would do well not to fall into such a snare.

But a Government may employ indirect agency and demand a share in the profit of a function which no one can distinctly claim as his own, and which naturally falls to the State as supreme over all public actions. Banks are the only institutions with whom it can negotiate for the performance of this service; for banks alone can deal with the funds received in exchange for the bank-notes and employ them. By such an arrangement the nation obtains the full benefit of the difference of cost between the two tools, gold and paper. The wealth saved by using the paper tool of exchange, by means of a bank, is retained in the country as capital, reproducing itself incessantly in the products it creates. Here we discover how and within what limit the issues of convertible bank-notes can benefit trade, and find means for merchants wherewith to carry out their operations. The fund which paper issues supply for this purpose is the payment made by the public when it purchases these notes. I say purchases, for bank-notes are as much bought and paid for by the public as sugar or corn, or as the gold which, but for the notes, would have been purchased from the miners. An issuing bank, unless it is faithless to the law of its business, advances these funds to customers on loan, or—far more commonly and usefully—on the discount of commercial bills. With the supply of purchasing power thus obtained on discount the merchant can buy, and those who sell are benefited. This, in very truth, is to employ the property which would have gone to purchase gold currency, but which is saved to the nation by the substitution of paper, as capital in the true economical sense of the term. It is wealth employed in producing other wealth. But this advantage has a limit: it cannot extend beyond the fund which the public by buying the bank-notes places at the disposal of the issuing bankers. Those amongst the public who use bank-notes paid to the bankers as much as they would have paid to the miners; the notes and the coin are both bought alike; but the property given for the notes, through the agency of the bankers, is placed in hands which apply it to industry as capital, and thus supports and enriches the nation, in addition to the currency service rendered by the paper substitutes.

The question now arises, Is a bank entitled to issue

bank-notes without control under the sole liability of paying them on demand, or is the State summoned to require security that the means of redemption shall be forthcoming when demanded? In the case of a bill or any other debt the State does not interfere with perfect freedom of contract. It does not say to a debtor that when he borrows he must pledge some definite property which will render the creditor safe. Is not the liability of the banker's fortune to its utmost extent sufficient also for his bank-note? It was not long ago the universal practice in England to emit bank-notes on this responsibility alone. The circulation of English country bank-notes, as well as those of Scotland and Ireland, rests on no other foundation. No one is bound to take the country banker's or the Scotchman's bank-notes; but if he does, the law gives him no other help than what it affords to every other debt. It will compel the debtor to pay with his property; but it takes no care that he shall have any property at all. Upon what principle, then, should an exception be made for bank-notes? Why should it provide for them property which is certain to pay them? On a principle upon which State intervention is constantly exercised and justified. It is this: that when the public is practically incompetent to protect itself, the State is warranted in coming to its aid with special legislation. Thus, in the manufacture of gun-barrels, in the moving and storing of gun-powder, in the management of passenger vessels, the minting of coin, the loading of ships, and other like matters, the law steps in with restrictions, sometimes with total prohibitions, and no one contests the propriety of its action. The issuing of bank-notes falls under this principle: the public is incompetent to enforce the safety which is necessary for the general good. The law gives no such help to a man who deposits his means with a banker, or accepts a bill or a cheque in payment. These are voluntary acts; the receiver or depositor knows perfectly well that he is bound to consider the honesty and the security of the man whom he trusts. It is otherwise with a shopkeeper who is offered the bank-notes which circulate all over the town, and still more so, with the person to whom a small bank-note is paid. He is under a semi-compulsion to take them. If the shopkeeper gives trouble by declining to take the ordinary currency, he runs the risk of losing his customer, who turns away to another shop or store. Bank-notes circulate largely among the poor and uneducated, and when the bank breaks, the loss is severe and distressing. These facts supply ample warrant to the State to require of issuing bankers, not only that they shall pay their debts to the utmost extent of their fortunes, as any other person, but further that they shall lodge such security as shall always provide for the payment of the debt acknowledged on the note.

A guarantee for the solvency of the notes may be obtained in various ways, but none seems so natural and so simple as a deposit of Government securities with some office of the State. It combines two advantages —safety, and a natural and fitting profit for the banker from the interest accruing on the bonds or stock. The old Exchequer Bill of the English Government was an excellent specimen of this kind of security. It could always be paid in for taxes, bore a daily interest, and was thoroughly trusted, and with reason, by the whole community. England has dealt with the problem on the principle here laid down in the Bank Charter Act of 1844; but as this statute will require special discussion, it is best not to break ground upon it in this place.

And now we reach the very critical question — In what numbers will convertible bank-notes circulate? It is the crucial question to test the soundness of every theory of currency. All who talk and write on currency are bound to push this question home to their minds, and not be content till they have framed for themselves a definite and intelligible answer.

Mr Tooke discerned the true answer; Mr Mill, with some little wavering, saw the light; but the general literature on money matters profoundly ignores the fact. The answer is the same as that which has already been given to the parallel question respecting coin. So many bank-notes as the public has a distinct want for will circulate, and no more. It is the universal law of all commodities in use, the law of demand and supply. Neither bankers, nor Parliament, nor suspensions of the Bank

Act, nor the need of borrowers, but the wants and convenience of the public, its willingness to hold bank-notes, the number and amount of the specific payments which bank-notes accomplish, with a certain spare stock as for all articles in use, can determine how many convertible bank-notes will remain in circulation, and not be returned upon the bankers for payment. This is the truth of truths for a convertible paper currency. This is so obvious a consequence of the fact that bank-notes are tools, and that their quantity will be regulated by the specific work which there is for them to do, that it almost seems a platitude to proclaim it; yet the whole array of traders and writers on money refuse to see this patent truth. They all believe, for instance, that to set free the issue of Bank of England notes by the Suspension of the Act of 1844 enables any amount of these notes to be issued at pleasure. They refuse to perceive and to learn.

An inflated circulation of bank-notes payable on demand is a pure absurdity, nothing better than nonsense. It would be just as sensible to speak of an inflated circulation of hats. It is easy for a hatter to make more hats than can be sold; but where would be the inflation in that case? In the number of hats circulating about the town?—in each man having a dozen hats in his house? The very question is puerile; there would be an inflation of hats, but it would be found in the shops of the hatters, not in the circulation of hats. Let any one ask himself how he can inflate his own use of bank-notes? Why should any one keep bank-notes which he cannot employ in a desk or till? He can buy with them, is the universal answer; but if he has already machinery enough with cheques, bills, and the ordinary supply of notes suited to his wants for purchasing, how can he need more? True, it is replied; but a banker can lend them to a man who has no money, and with them he can buy or meet his engagements in the day of difficulty. That is so, no doubt; but unhappily for the banker, the man to whom his borrower pays them has already as many notes as his business requires; the excess now pouring in upon him he either himself, or indirectly through his banker, sends in to the issuing bank, which finds to its cost that it has lent, not bank-notes which remain out in circulation, but the funds wherewith it has to redeem these surplus lent notes, which instantly come back upon it for payment. And so, in actual fact, in the time of crisis, borrowers do not take away their loans in bank-notes; they receive authority from the lending bank to draw cheques upon it, which are settled at the Clearing House without any cash passing. The Bank of England never has been so absurd as to say to a distressed borrower, "You shall have assistance, only you must take it out in notes;" yet this would have been its language if it had believed that it could increase its means of lending by getting additional bank-notes out into circulation. It knows perfectly well that the notes would return upon it in a few hours for payment. Those who had received the bank-notes from the persons to whom the Bank had lent them would at once place them to the credit of their accounts, either directly with the Bank of England, or with their own bankers, who would pass them on, as unwanted, to their credit with the Bank. They then would draw cheques on the Bank to meet purchases or to make payments; and the final result would be that the Bank had got back the bank-notes, but would be obliged to face these cheques out of its other resources. The forcing the borrowers to take the loan in bank-notes would have done the Bank no good; it would have made a simple loan precisely as if these bank-notes had never existed. No issuer of notes can by any possibility add to his resources and powers of lending by means of convertible notes, except to the extent that the public will keep them in circulation, and will not present them to him for payment.

An elaborate circular of a Chamber of Commerce lays down that "to restrict the supply of bank-notes is to stifle commerce. A contracted circulation raises prices. A limitation on the issue of notes raises the rate of interest charged by bankers on discounting merchants' bills." These are the universal ideas of traders; but where do they get these fine principles from? Not from science, nor from analysis of the facts which they claim, as practical men, peculiarly to understand; they must be primitive truths, dawning on the mercantile mind by intuition, and shining by their own transparent light. There are many assumptions involved in this language, and much ignorance too. How can the want of bank-notes stifle commerce? Commerce is the exchanging of goods; the bank-note is one of its tools; but it gives no increase of wealth nor of buying power; it is but a piece of paper; what it does is to give to the banker buying power which he can lend to a borrower. But where does the banker get this buying power from? Not from his own resources, certainly; he obtains it from the public. The real nature of the act of issuing notes is that the banker has first obtained property or the command of property, from a part of the public, his depositors. He then repays them with the notes, retaining the property; in other words, he gives in payment of the deposits another debt due by him to the holders of the notes—he pays a debt with another debt—and it is the holder of the notes who enables the banker to satisfy the demand of his depositor, and yet retain the property. The holder of the notes is the true lender through the bank to the man who obtains assistance, who borrows from the bank. But there is no increase of buying power in all this, not a particle of wealth or of lending power is created by it. Bank-notes are but intermediate agency. Their action consists in making the holder of the notes lend his spare property, not himself directly, but through the agency of a bank, to a man who wishes to borrow and to use it. Suppress the notes, the wealth of England will remain the same. Those who paid for them would have the same wealth at their disposal, the same disposition to lend, only the lending would be made through cheques instead of bank-notes, or by direct loan to borrowers. Commerce is not stifled or vitalised by notes; it only gets a convenient machine for exchanging wealth, but no increase of wealth except so far as coin would have had to be bought from a foreign miner.

We are next told that a contracted circulation raises prices; upon what evidence or principle does this favourite dogma rest? Bank-notes really convertible are identical in value with gold; the slightest difference of value between them would instantly bring the bank-notes to the issuer for gold. Nothing which happens to convertible notes can affect their value; the value of the gold must rise or fall before the notes can be touched. In fact, bank-notes may be regarded as tickets entitling the holder to obtain the gold out of the vault when he likes. An issue of notes smaller than what the public could employ and keep out in circulation means only an inconvenience really trifling; cheques and bills would be more freely used, and that would be the whole of the matter. A little more gold coin would perhaps be employed; but the quantity would be trifling, and the value of gold is determined, not in England, but in Europe generally, or rather over the whole world.

And then "to limit bank-notes is to raise the rate of

interest." But how? No doubt a banker by issuing notes procures more to lend to his customers; he can grant larger discount to those who bring him commercial bills. But the funds which he thus obtains to lend he acquires from the public. His notes enable him to lend more, but what he lends the public provides; there is no increase of things to lend. The rate of interest on loans and discounts depends on the spare capital which owners all over the country cannot employ themselves, but are willing to lend to others who can make use of it in trade and industry. A diminution of bank-notes does not make this spare capital smaller; it only places less of it at the disposal of the issuing banker. Bank-notes are but paper—paper tools—not the property or capital itself. Interest does not depend on more or fewer tools of paper being used, but on wealth available for lending. Banking, with all its machinery of bank-notes, cheques, bills, and the like, is only intermediate agency; the only thing it does is—not to create property, but simply to place it in different hands. There is only one case in which an issue of bank-notes might tell on interest, and that is in a particular spot, at a special time, and under stated circumstances, in a panic in the money market. Whether such an issue is possible, and if so, under what conditions, will be discussed in the next chapter.

Section II.—The Bank Charter Act of 1844.

THIS seems to be the fitting place for explaining the manner in which bank-notes are issued in England, more especially under the Statute of 1844, which re-organised the issues of the Bank of England, and made provision for the ultimate condition of the paper currency of England.

Up to the passing of this Act, it was open to any bank or private person to put forth bank-notes. One condition only was imposed as a guarantee of their value. They were required to be convertible, payable on demand. Not to pay a bank-note on presentation was an act of bankruptcy, and the issuer passed at once under the laws of insolvency.

There probably has never existed a law whose meaning has been so vehemently and incessantly disputed, and is disputed still, as the Bank Charter Act of 1844. No one has accused it of obscurity of language: what it prescribes is most simple, easy to be understood, and equally easy of execution. No one raises a question as to what is legal, and what not, under its provisions: yet the significance of the Statute, what its enactments effect or do not effect, whether it is a revolution or a beneficial law, are matters of the most differing and most bitter interpretation. It is regarded as the destroyer or the saviour of trade.

In examining the nature of this Statute, let us pursue

the method adopted by all judges in considering an Act of Parliament in a Court of Law. They take no notice of speeches delivered in Parliament by its authors. What they aimed at, what they supposed the measure they advocated to enjoin, counts for nothing, if the language of the law is clear. The Court looks at what the Statute says, and at nothing else: from that the Court learns what it is. We will follow this path, examining each point that presents itself.

1. The Act divides the Bank of England into two departments, one the Banking Department, the other the Issue Department. The latter is exclusively concerned with the issuing of notes. That operation is carried out under fixed rules laid down in the Statute—and the vital point to observe here is that the corporation called the Bank of England has no voice, discretion, or control over the issues. In the Issue Department the Bank Directors have no more authority or right to speak or act than any other person in the kingdom. The Banking Department is the Bank of England, pure and simple, as private a bank as any other bank in the country. As such, as a private bank, it possesses two advantages: a very big customer in the Government account, and a special benefit from the bank-notes conferred on it by the law.

2. The Act limits the quantity of bank-notes issued by private banks in the nation to the quantity existing at the time when the Act became law. If any of these

private issuers cease to issue, the bank-notes assigned to them lapse, and the amount of the whole private issue becomes permanently reduced by nearly that amount.

3. The Bank of England, the private bank so called, is authorised to receive from the Issue Department fourteen millions of notes, with a certain proportion of the lapsed private issues, as they lapse. The quantity stands now at about fifteen millions. These bank-notes the Bank receives from the Issue Department—(which, in reality, is an office of the State)—on the condition that it shall give gold for them to the public, whenever they are presented for payment. Of course this fact may be regarded as meaning that the Bank of England is a direct issuer of notes to the extent of fifteen millions, but it is far simpler and truer to look upon the Bank as a receiver, for special reasons, of so many notes from the sole issuer, the office of the State called the Issue Department. The Bank is subject to the further condition that it shall invest these fifteen millions in securities on which it receives the interest. They are invested at three per cent.

4. Bank of England notes are declared to be legal tender everywhere except at the Bank itself. The Bank cannot pay its debts with bank-notes, as being legal tender. Any of its creditors may decline them.

5. Every note is payable at the premises of the Bank of England—some out of its private resources, the remainder at the State office, called the Issue Depart-

ment. The law further enacts that all the notes issued by the Issue Department beyond the fifteen millions, shall be covered for this payment by a deposit of gold kept in the Department. The whole issue thus consists of two parts: one, now fifteen millions, assigned to the Bank of England, and payable by it, the remainder put forth by the Issue Department in exchange for gold given to it by the public, and kept permanently in the vault to guarantee convertibility.

Such are the main provisions of this much-debated statute—it remains now to ascertain their practical significance.

1. In the first place it is obvious that it sentences the private issues in England to extinction by a process of greater or less duration. Many causes are ever at work causing private banks to cease issuing; sometimes leading partners die, and the bank comes to an end, or, as was the case recently with the National Provincial Bank of England, a bank voluntarily abandons country issues in order to acquire the right of carrying on banking in London, a privilege refused by law to joint-stock banks issuing bank-notes. It is obviously the intention of the statute that ultimately Bank of England notes shall be the only paper currency of England. This intention is further marked by the privilege of legal tender (save always at the Bank itself) granted exclusively to the Bank of England.

2. Ultimately the bank-notes, uncovered by an actual

lodgment of gold to secure convertibility, will be limited to the amount which will accrue to the Bank of England when all the private issues shall have disappeared, but the solvency and convertibility of these particular notes will be secured by the investment in securities to their amount required by the Act.

Many suppose that the debt of fourteen millions due by the Government to the Bank—which we may presume was the reason why the line between the uncovered and the covered issues was drawn at fourteen millions—is specially appropriated as a security for payment to the uncovered issues emitted by the bank on its own liability, so that in the event of the bank's insolvency there will be a special asset of that amount for the uncovered notes; but it is extremely doubtful whether this view is sound in law. The point is not decided, nor is it likely to be.

3. Uncovered notes are restricted in amount. They cannot exceed fifteen millions now. Any quantity of notes above this amount may be obtained from the Issue Department, but they must be purchased with gold, and that gold kept locked up in the office. Absolute restriction, therefore, there is none—the public may have as many notes as it pleases; but it must pay with gold, for all above fifteen millions. No portion of the whole issue is available for lending either on discount to traders, or by loans and advances. What the bank receives from the public, the fifteen millions, must be invested in securities; the

gold given for all above is stored away in the vault of the Issue Department.

4. The gold stored and kept in the Government Office, the Issue Department, in no sense whatever belongs to the Bank of England. It is no part of its reserve, and it is a great misfortune that the framers of the Act of 1844 should have made the exceedingly unintelligent blunder of mixing up together in the weekly reports of the bullion at the Bank, two absolutely dissimilar and distinct things—the gold stored away by one office to face the bank-notes, and the gold belonging to the Bank of England as a banker. The gold at the State's office lies under self-acting rules. It may be said to belong to an automaton,—so many more notes out, so much more gold in store, or the reverse. The fluctuations of the notes denote that the public is buying fewer or more notes with gold, nothing more. Fluctuations, on the contrary, in the bank-notes held by the Banking Department, are genuine changes in the reserve of a private bank, and alone should be subject to banking discussions as to the state of the Bank, the rate of interest, and other kindred matters.

5. The figure which divides the issues resting on the Bank's liability and those for which gold is actually stored, has great importance. It was laid down in the Act at fourteen millions, upon no deeper reason probably than that this sum was due by the State to the Bank, and that a vague notion prevailed at the time that this debt was

specially assigned as a security for the notes. The lapse of private issues raises the figure as time rolls on. The important practical point is to ascertain the figure up to which the public will retain the notes issued and never present them for payment in the worst of crises. From the nature of things only a rough approximation to this limit can be made; but this much is ascertained fact, that since the passing of the Act the public has never asked for payment in cash of any notes beyond those for which the automaton, the State Office, had gold ready in hand to give; not one of the uncovered notes, which the Bank of England was liable for, has been presented. There has never been since 1844 the slightest tendency of a run upon the Bank for the payment of a single one of the fifteen millions of notes. Gold, no doubt, is constantly asked for at the counters of the Bank; but what does the Bank do? It sends the notes over to the State Office, and gets gold for them at once; but the stock of the Issue Department has never been exhausted. The Directors of the Bank of England have never been called upon in the worst times to give a thought about providing gold for the uncovered notes. These fifteen millions, so far, have proved to have been founded on a rock, and are covered either by gold or securities. The currency of England is thus shown to be of the very strongest: a gold currency for every practically possible demand, and a paper currency purchased by the public for which the public has a constant and unbroken demand.

6. Lastly the great principle is observed that the profits of the issues shall at least be shared with the State, and not be the exclusive benefit of a private banker. The Bank, we are informed by Mr Thompson Hankey, pays nearly £200,000 a year to Government for the fifteen millions of notes which it issues on its own liability. Its own profit from this source, after deducting expenses of management, amounts to about £100,000. Thus the State reaps from the issues double the profit of that earned by the Bank.

And now, what is the final judgment to be passed on this much-disputed law? In respect of the supposed aims of its promoters, it must be pronounced a failure. It failed, because they sought to perform the impossible. They framed it as a machine to act on the amount of the paper currency of the country, to be a self-acting contrivance for enlarging or contracting the circulation, according as gold flowed into, or ebbed away from, England. The Act, there is reason to believe, was designed as a remedy against drains, an impracticable scheme founded on a real ignorance of the nature and laws of currency. It proposed to regulate the amount of the currency by law. Inflation would be prevented, for issues which had to be bought with gold could never be excessive. Thus wild emissions of bank-notes, consequent speculation and rise of prices, high discounts, drains of gold leaving the country, and the offspring of all these evils, panics, crises, bankruptcies, and ruin would be averted. All this was to be done by a self-acting machine, that nicely adapted its corrective action to the precise maladies of the money-market. Alas! these wonderful effects never came to pass; they proved to be only dreams of the imagination. Panics have been as severe since 1844 as before. The fluctuations of the rate of discount have been as violent; speculative joint-stock companies, works commenced on credit,—destroying capital and with no means for completion,—depression and elevation of stocks and shares, bankruptcies and commercial paralyses which have required years to heal, have reached, under this cunningly devised Act, heights of extravagance previously unknown. The Bank Act was as helpless as a baby to counteract the mischief, for the very simple reason that these matters lay clean out of its reach: it had no hands wherewith to touch them. Its authors did not know that the quantity of a metallic or of a convertible paper currency in circulation is determined by the number of those particular transactions—that buying and selling, including, of course, bankers' reserves, as being currency at work—which employ ready money; and that it is the public, so wanting and so using ready money, be it coin or bank-notes, which regulates the number of these tools of exchange which shall be used, and not the law, nor issuing bankers, nor any other extraneous force or authority. The law, of course, may forbid the public from having as many notes as it would otherwise buy and employ; it may amend the Act of 1844, and declare that there shall be ten millions of bank-notes in England, and no more. The effect of that would be to increase vastly the use of cheques, which would be only the substitution of one piece of banking paper for another, or it might compel more coin to be bought from miners, which would be a diminution of the national capital; but it would not touch speculation. Nor was this what the parents of the Statute had in their minds. They thought of a machine which should act on the voluntary employment of notes by the public, and thereby control mercantile operations. But a gigantic speculation, covering the whole English trade, with its rise of prices and its crashes, may be carried on without requiring a single additional bank-note, if ready-money transactions—which are always relatively few—are not altered. The Issue Department cannot act on loans, discounts and rates of interest, except so far as it fixes the figure at which the storing of gold commences too low. If the public would keep out permanently in circulation twenty millions, without ever presenting one for payment, then the loan and discount market loses five millions of means; but this would be a permanent unchanging diminution of its resources made once for all, affecting all times, and utterly unconnected with oscillating movements. The nation would be so much the poorer permanently by the needless purchase of gold. That would be the only result; and this is the only way in which the Issue Department can come in contact with the money-market and the rate of interest.

Is, then, the figure fifteen millions the proper one, or is it too low? This is an issue of fact, and facts will supply the answer. On three several occasions, in 1847, 1857, and 1866, the Act was suspended—that is, repealed for the time, and the Bank of England was free to issue as many notes as it chose, without storing up corresponding gold in its vault. Under these circumstances did the Bank, which had recovered its unrestricted liberty to issue, put into circulation more uncovered notes than would have been possible without suspension? The answer supplied by facts is, with a trifling exception in 1857, NO: and the answer is crushing and decisive. The exception in 1857 was £800,000, an unimportant sum in a great crisis. This exception would not have occurred had the line stood then where it does now, at fifteen millions. The demonstration is complete that the Act does not restrict. It does not diminish by a single pound the quantity of bank-notes, which, but for it, the public would obtain without buying them with gold. After the suspensions, the weekly reports of the Bank constantly proclaimed that the quantity which the Act would have required for the Issue Department was there through the spontaneous action of the public. The suspensions of the Act were thus shown to be nullities. The sole enactment of the statute which could restrict was the requirement that beyond the fifteen millions gold must be given for notes; the requirement was suspended, yet every pound of gold demanded by the Act was at the Bank. The suspension did nothing whatever, because with it or without it the required quantity of gold was lodged at the Bank.

Such is the proof of the nullity of Suspension; yet the belief in its virtues is as widely spread and as flourishing as ever. Currency is a matter of feeling with the banking world and its oracles; what contradicts feeling and improvised theory is passed by unheeded, but men who know what science is think and speak otherwise. Professor Sumner, in his able work on American currency, states plainly that the nullity of the effect of Suspension disposes of the charge brought against the Act of 1844, that it restricts. But this cannot be so, replies the City. How can it be said that the Act does not restrict, when veteran bankers and intelligent merchants in every commercial agony clamour for its suspension, and declare that they find from it instantaneous relief? To this the answer is simple: a charm often effects a cure. A phial of pure water, believed to be medicine, has often given relief to suffering patients; but is it water or the delusion which cures? A crisis in the money-market is a matter of alarm; wild uncertainty,—who is solvent? and who is going to fail?—terrifies every merchant and every banker. What so natural, then, as the conviction that bank-notes gushing forth in unchecked numbers will dispel the danger? Ignorance and imagination, set in motion by fright, may work miracles. The illusion, once imbibed, changes conduct at once. The frightened depositor or creditor, when he hears of the suspension, ceases to think about rushing to demand payment; the banker, under the same power of belief, lends less grudgingly. But there is no fact beneath this action, only imagination. A nullity, vivified by the imagination, can bring no lasting aid. Let us listen to Mr Patterson, speaking of the crisis of 1866:—"The panic was at its height at mid-day. Shortly before one o'clock the second editions of the daily papers announced that the Bank Act was suspended. A salutary change became possible, and the crowds in the adjoining streets diminished. The run slackened; but the announcement was premature. The Bank Act was not suspended, nor indeed at that time had the Government given any attention to the matter. In this emergency a deputation from the joint-stock and private banks was despatched to apprise the Government of the state of matters in the City, and to urge the immediate suspension of the Act of 1844. In the City the managers and directors of banks and other monetary establishments remained at their post till past midnight, anxiously receiving tidings of disaster, and waiting for the announcement of the suspension of the Act. It was midnight before the announcement was made. The effect of the announcement was so salutary, that next day (Saturday) it was thought that the crisis was at an end." Can picture be more graphic?—the terrified and ignorant crowds waiting for the angel to come and trouble the water, and the instantaneous relief when he came. But was it a cure? Let us hearken to the next words of Mr Patterson:—"But, as became visible in a day or two, the crisis was not at an end." How could it? The suspension did not give a note more to the agonised borrowers than they would have had without it. Helpless terror and unreasoning ignorance could not farther go.

Restriction and suspension being swept away, the Bank Charter Act of 1844 comes forth in all its simplicity. It is a good Act, but not in the sense conceived by its authors. It gives to the nation a perfectly protected paper currency, part of it by actual gold in hand, part by the securities in which the Bank is required to place what it receives for its portion of the notes. The nation saves the fifteen millions of capital which it would have cost to purchase metallic tools. The nullity of suspension proves that the Act inflicts no injury on the money-market. The nation receives twice as much profit from the issues as the Bank. The purchase of fifteen millions of securities by the Bank sets free that amount of capital to take its part in the production of wealth. Two amendments would render the Act complete. The office of issue ought to be placed in Somerset House or Whitehall; the world would then understand that the State is the real issuer.

And, secondly, in the weekly reports, the bullion which belongs to the Issue Department should be kept strictly apart from the bullion which belongs to the Bank of England as a private banker.

One point more remains to be noticed. Of what denomination ought notes to be? Much opposition is directed in England against small notes, but it has its roots in prejudice and not in science. The size of notes is a question of convenience, coupled with the importance of guarding against forgery. One-pound notes are eminently prosperous in Scotland; they are even preferred to sovereigns. In Austria, Italy, and America, notes much smaller than those of one pound circulate freely and successfully. No objection is heard against them, except when very small; they are then apt to become dirty, defaced, and capable of being easily forged. The denomination of notes is analogous to that of cheques. Very small cheques cause bankers much trouble and clerical work; they are consequently disliked. One-pound notes were suppressed in England by an act of panic and ignorance. In 1825 many issuing banks became insolvent, and their one-pound notes, which were widely spread in retail business, brought grievous loss to many poor persons. The denomination of bank-notes was consequently limited to five-pounds. It was not perceived that the loss arose, not from the size of the note, but the badness of the issuer, and that the objection lay against any notes, of whatever kind being issued by such untrustworthy agency.

We must not bid farewell to the Bank Charter Act of 1844 without mentioning a wonderful doctrine propounded in connection with it by persons who claim to possess the highest authority on currency. The greatest stress is laid upon this doctrine as expressing the fundamental principle which ought to govern all currencies which are composed of coin and convertible bank-notes mixed together. It is believed that this doctrine was reckoned by those who were supposed to be the advisers of Sir Robert Peel to be the brilliant discovery of the grand secret which gives soundness to a mixed circulation; but this cannot be affirmed with certainty. But however that may be, this principle is fondly held, and strenuously proclaimed, by great personages, by Chancellors of the Exchequer in and out of Parliament, by Secretaries of State laying down rules for the currencies of important colonies and dependencies, and by countless writers who speak authoritatively on currency. This doctrine affirms that a mixed currency of coin and paper should be made to circulate in the same quantity as if it had been purely metallic. Had the assertion been that the mixed currency should be made throughout of the same quality as the purely metallic, it would have been perfectly intelligible, and of unquestionable excellence. The framers of the Bank Act might have fairly boasted that they had carried it out into execution—that the currency of England contained bank-notes which were as good, as trustworthy, as sound guarantees of value as the sovereigns which circulated by their side. But to make the numbers of a mixed currency the same as if the currency had been all of sovereigns—that indeed, the ex-Lord Mayor might have said, passes the human understanding.

We need not dwell on the questions—first, How in the world any one is to find out whether the bank-notes of a mixed currency are more or fewer than the sovereigns which would have been used, had there been no bank-notes? and, secondly, Having found this out, by what process he is to force the public to take more notes to fill up the deficiency, or to surrender the excess which it has contrived to get into its hands? Nor need we challenge the inventors of this doctrine to explain their conception of the nature of currency, or the possibility of making any one, except the public itself, the determiner of how many sovereigns and bank-notes it will buy and use; it is enough to ask them whether they imagine it to be possible to violate the law of gravity in coins and notes one particle more than in any other substance? Coins are heavy, bank-notes are light. Supposing these tools to be equally efficient, equally trusted, can it be conceived that the public would employ as many of the heavy as of the light ones? Can any one believe that if the twenty millions and more of Bank of England notes were suppressed altogether, as many sovereigns would be asked for to supply their places? Every day men carry about their persons bank-notes worth thousands, even hundreds of thousands, of pounds; would they ever be willing to carry as many sovereigns? What an opportunity for thieves—the visible and tempting bags, instead of the invisible bank-notes. Is it not obvious that the extinction of the Bank of England notes would be followed by a huge increase of cheques? Poor currency! hard indeed is its fate. The professors of its science teach palpable absurdity; the public is bewildered, and fails to understand; the oracles insist with gravity that they possess a science which is a mystery for the many; and the world pronounces currency to lie beyond the human understanding.

Section III.—Inconvertible Bank-Notes.

We have now reached the region where theory revels in all its forms: inconvertible bank-notes. Great Governments seize with avidity upon this form of currency as the means of reaping gain at the expense of the community, and then they justify their practice by throwing dust into the eyes of the public by the help of every kind of arbitrary and unscientific assertion. The subject deserves the closest examination.

An inconvertible bank-note is a paper tool of exchange which acknowledges on its face a debt to be due, which promises to pay it, but specifies no fixed time for the payment, and for which consequently the coin promised cannot be obtained on demand. The first thought which arises is the question : how is it that any one is willing to give away his property in exchange for such paper ? A convertible bank-note indeed is not payment, but the coin, which is payment, can be procured for the asking ; thus the guarantee it furnishes to a seller, that he shall be able to obtain other goods equal to those he has sold, is complete. A bank-note not payable on demand supplies no such guarantee ; it is not certain that it ever will be paid at all. It circulates for two reasons ; it is issued by the Government, and the belief is universal that a Government will never repudiate its liability, and will pay at last. But this belief, by itself alone, would not be sufficient to ensure a large and easy circulation for such paper guarantees, so Governments apply to them an instrument of great efficacy for attaining their end. They endow them with the right of legal tender ; they enact a law which compels every creditor who has debited a buyer with a dollar or pound to accept these notes as a full discharge of his debt. Upon such a basis the operation of issue becomes feasible. The Government owes interest on a national debt, and purchases supplies of all kinds from traders. It forces the national creditors to take these notes as payment of the interest due, and persuades contractors to supply them with goods by means of the knowledge that they will be able in turn to pass on these notes to all to whom they are indebted. Thus the notes come forth, and, once out, do not return upon the issuer.

2. The next fact to notice is that on one condition these notes, for which payment cannot be demanded at pleasure, circulate on a level of value with coin—the condition that their numbers shall not be in excess of the want of the public for these tools; that their supply shall not exceed the demand. In the case of coin, as we have seen, an excess of metallic dollars or sovereigns flows back at once to the strongholds for storing them, precisely as the farmer's ploughs in icy winter return to their sheds. In the same manner bank-notes payable on demand come back upon the issuers; no one wants them. But inconvertible bank-notes have no such machinery for adapting their numbers to the requirements of the public for them; once out in circulation, they are always out; there is no self-adjusting apparatus for them, as there is for the other tools of exchange. Now, it may well happen that the quantity of inconvertible notes issued is not greater than what the public requires; so it was with the Bank of England notes for several years, when it was forbidden by law to pay its notes in gold. Similarly in other countries excess has been often found to be very small. But what is excess? As with all tools, too many for the work they have to do; and it has been shown that that work is to effect those exchanges, that buying and paying, in which each particular tool is employed. Ready

money payments are the work to be performed; and if these payments do not increase, whilst the stock of bank-notes circulating is enlarged, then there is excess.

3. But what is the test of the existence of excess, or to use popular language, of inflation? What effect is generated which leads to the discovery of its cause? A fall in the value of the paper compared with the value of the coin which it acknowledges to be due. The supply of them is too great; many persons have more of them than they know what to do with; to get rid of them they are willing to part with them at a reduced value. It may be difficult to specify the case of a definite holder of them who goes through this process of thinking, and then resolves to reckon them as worth less; but it is impossible to doubt that this is what takes place in practical life, and that the depreciation of the notes, whether expressed in the United States by the premium which gold bears compared with paper dollars, or, as formerly in England, by the discount attached to the notes, is the result purely of an excess of supply, which lowers the value of all commodities alike. Each additional issue adds to the depreciation and to the disorder which it creates in all money transactions. The notes are worth less and less.

4. Thus, an inconvertible bank-note becomes tainted with the worst vice which a currency can possess—unsteadiness of value. It purchases more or else less of the same goods at different times. We know that the

essence of a good currency is, that it should give to the man who takes it a reliable assurance that he shall be able with it to procure other goods of the same value with those which he has given away : an inconvertible bank-note deliberately corrupts and vitiates that assurance. He is not sure that he will not incur special loss through the bank-note currency, a loss intended by neither buyer nor seller, but not the less real on that account. The debasement of the tool of exchange is an annoying and mischievous nuisance, thrust into a region from which it should be rigorously excluded, the exchanging of the necessaries and enjoyments required by civilization. It is thrust in for a motive absolutely unconnected with the sole purpose for which any currency exists and passes into universal use. It is as wanton a perversion of a most indispensable tool as if any one were to impart to the blade of a knife a quality which would make it sharp or blunt capriciously. The change in the nature of the currency tells on every price in every shop or store—for price is only the quantity of currency computed to be equal to the value of the goods. The more civilized a nation is, the vaster the development of its trade, the larger the number of debts to be settled and stipulated annuities to be continuously paid, the more disastrous is the violence done to the currency, the more injurious its consequences to society. Every sale on credit is converted into gambling, and what but pure harm can come from adding an inevitable element of gambling to every shopkeeper's accounts, to every bill which moves the operations of commerce, to every purchase of a house or farm which covenants for the payment of a rent of so many dollars or pounds for a number of years, to every man who lives by the interest of the national debt of the country? And no small part of the evil hence resulting is the necessity imposed on traders to add to the natural price of their goods as a protection against the risks consequent on the corruption of the public money. Most of all is this felt in foreign trade. The Englishman or German who sends a cargo of goods to America, knows that he will be paid with bills expressed in dollars: he cannot tell what will be the value of the dollar when the bills become due: he protects himself by exacting from the American buyer a stiffer price.

And it is no small part of the calamity and disgrace of an inconvertible currency that it leads to large and incessant violation of contracts. Every stipulated sum which has to be paid with such notes is one thing to-day and another thing to-morrow. The essence of honour and good faith in contracts, as well as of trustworthy trade, is to give the thing covenanted; but in the place of that stipulated value the nominal paper dollar specified is given, as if that was the payment agreed upon. But what does the unhappy receiver discover? That he has been defrauded—that the paper dollar he gets will not buy as much as the dollar he stipulated—that prices have gone up in every store—and that he is injured in purse and property. In raising prices storekeepers are impelled by necessity. Real prices are not altered; the sellers ask for more dollars, but as every dollar is worth less, the larger number of dollars now brings them only the same value, when it becomes their turn to buy goods with them. Every creditor who is paid in the paper dollar encounters these raised prices, and finds that a portion of his property has been confiscated.*

These public misfortunes are summed up in the fact that no one is able to say what a dollar is. A dollar becomes a word whose meaning no one knows: it must be sought from the price of gold in paper dollars. The dollar has a new meaning on each succeeding day: it is one thing to-day, another to-morrow: is it possible for a currency, whose one and only function is to enable to buy with certainty as much as was sold, to possess a greater vice?

It might be a wonder that such a dollar should have any value—that any one should be willing to give his goods for it. The reason for its having value is that the paper has written upon it a promise that the United States will give a dollar—plainly a metallic dollar—for it, and it is this belief that at some time the United

* Some of the details of the injuries wrought by an inconvertible currency are given with great vigour in a very able and admirable "Address delivered at Omaha by Professor A. L. Perry, of Williams College." They will be found in the Appendix.

States will make good their word which induces the public to attach value to the greenback. The public faith is pledged; the responsibility thence arising on the Government for all the evils which the paper dollar inflicts on society thus becomes only too clear.

5. The usual defence pleaded for inconvertible bank-notes is necessity, the political distress of the hour. The State is in urgent want of means, the limits of taxation have been reached. What else can a government do under such circumstances but procure what it imperiously requires with promises to pay at some future time? It may be so. On this principle national debts may be justified. The State, in its day of need, obtains wealth from the country on credit, and consumes it; in return, it gives an annuity to the lenders. In such a transaction there is one injury—the destruction of the wealth borrowed; but the injury occurs once only, and then it ends. Not so with inconvertible notes. In common with a national debt, an issue of inconvertible bank-notes obtains and consumes a country's wealth without payment; but a mischief in addition is set to work which never stops. As long as an inconvertible currency lasts, it never ceases to harass trade and every commercial dealing between man and man. The harm is renewed day after day, week after week, year after year; and all the while the State is gaining from all this disorder nothing proportionate to the mischief created. There is no counterbalancing advantage to the Govern-

ment to compensate the loss which the country suffers. The Government created the inconvertible note as a tax on which it saves interest, and gathered the tax once for all ; but a bad, unsound, untrustworthy currency persecutes society at every turn and brings loss on all but gamblers. It poisons every sale as the days roll on, every exchange ; and what is human life but making and exchanging ?

The moral which these facts teach is clear. Overwhelming necessity may excuse the original imposition of so easy but so vicious a tax, but the pressure once over, not an hour should be lost by any legislature who has any knowledge of the nature and working of money, to arrest the plague and sweep away inconvertible paper.

But, reply many persons in every country, most of all in the United States, trade rises or falls with the abundance or scarcity of money. Plenty of money means lively business—buyers abound. What can they do with their money but buy with it ? It will walk into every store, every shop. Borrowers, when money is plentiful, will find it easy then to obtain the means for carrying on an expanding trade. Is it not notorious that liberty to issue cheapens discount, because it enables a banker, at no cost to himself, to place means of buying in the hands of his friends ? There cannot be too much money—who ever heard of such a thing ? It is easy to speak of inflation, but it remains true all the same, that the man who has bank-notes in his pocket, be they inflated or not, can buy, and that the banker can shower these notes upon him at less than six cents a-piece.

That such fallacies should be uttered in the nineteenth century is astonishing. First of all, such language does not know that currency is only a tool, that money is not the thing which really buys, but only an instrument used in buying. It is the property with which money is itself bought that buys. Buying is only exchanging goods, absolutely nothing else; to sell for money is only double barter in the place of single barter. Money does not, directly, produce a single particle of wealth, nor create any additional power of buying which would not exist without it; it only places wealth in different hands. An issuing banker or Government may by the help of a piece of paper take property out of one man's disposal and put it in another's; but without the bank-note, that property would be exchanged, that is, would buy and sell, just the same. Money cannot create increase of trade, unless, if coin, it is obtained as a gift from the miners, then of course the country which receives the present could with it get more wealth from some other nation; but if the gift is in coin and remains coin, then the nation, though getting it for nothing, would not be one particle the richer, supposing that already its currency was full. With respect to bank-notes, their action is to procure property from one section of the public and transfer it to another. If the notes are irredeemable, the issuer, if a Government, has acquired and consumed a portion of the nation's wealth—there is less property for trade, less for exchanging. If the issuer is a private banker, he and his friend to whom he lends it on discount have taken away property from the holders of the bank-notes, and employ it for their own purposes. With that property, of course, they can and do trade; but if it had been left with the public, the goods of which it consists would have been exchanged, would have been bought and sold just the same. There is no increase of wealth or of trade for the whole country. No motive can be derived from the language here examined for inflicting on a nation the intolerable mischief of gambling and uncertainty imported into every commercial transaction by a tool of exchange corrupted by incessant fluctuations of value. At all times and in every place, there is one paramount quality of a currency that can do its work, that it shall be able to buy goods worth those that have been sold.

But another mischief is exceedingly apt to be developed under an inconvertible paper currency. When banks are employed as the instruments of its issue, experience overwhelmingly shows that good banking tends to disappear. Bankers, by the help of such notes, obtain resources so easily that they become excited and careless of prudence. They lend themselves to fostering speculation, to promoting wild companies, to making roads in the wilderness which cannot repay for years the wealth destroyed in constructing them, and to other like operations. When the day of reckoning arrives at last, it is discovered that a large part of what was obtained from the public has been lost for ever, whilst the baneful unstable currency remains. Well might Mr Greene, as quoted by Mr Edward Atkinson, exclaim, when speaking of the consequences of the Legal Tender Act, "Speculation ran riot, every form of wastefulness and extravagance prevailed in town and country, nowhere more than in Philadelphia, under the very eyes of Congress—luxury of dress, luxury of equipage, luxury of the table. We are told of an entertainment at which £800 were spent in pastry. As I read of the private letters of those days, I sometimes feel as a man might feel on looking down on a foundering ship whose crew were preparing for death by breaking open the steward's room and drinking themselves into madness." The Legal Tender currency placed the nation's wealth in the hands of destroyers.

What is a dollar? it has been seen is the question which an inconvertible currency cannot answer. Most correctly and humorously exclaims Mr Atkinson, "Why not say the greenback? A dollar is a piece of gold or silver which we have outgrown. The only use of notes is to buy with; why not, instead of printing on paper, 'The United States—One Dollar,' print, The United States, one turkey, one roast pig, or one horse; and for small change, The United States, one newspaper, and make them a legal tender, promising to convert them into bonds at 3·65 interest, which interest of course would not be paid in gold, for gold is esteemed a useless, mischievous tyrant, out of date, fit only to be exported or banished, fit for foreign paupers, but entirely played out in enlightened America. If it is proposed to pay interest in gold on the inconvertible bonds, the specie standard is admitted, and the whole case is given up. If it is proposed to pay the interest in inconvertible notes, then the proposal—(to exchange the notes for bonds at 3·65)—is only to swop worthless pieces of stamped paper, one for another."

In the same sense remarks *The Financier* of New York of July 3, 1875, an Economical journal second to none in any country for ability and clearness of thinking: "As for the only consistent and honest mode of inflation—not yet proposed, because it *is* such a mode—that of discarding the promissory form and issuing tokens of paper, rubber, leather, or any convenient material, and stamping them 'One Dollar,' 'United States of America,' under the constitutional power of Congress to coin money, the inflationist would not exchange the meanest thing he has for such money, although he could not consistently refuse."

It is a marvellous thing that so gross a delusion as the supposition that a reality is given to the paper dollar by granting it an interest payable in another piece of paper should have taken so strong a hold on men's minds in many parts of America—that so acute a people should not have perceived that it was to explain, *Ignotum per ignotum*. It does not occur to them that the vital question to ask of every currency is—What is its power of buying? will it do its work, and upon what principle?

The conclusion is irresistible: an inconvertible currency is incapable of being defended. It may have had an excusable origin in an overwhelming political situation, and if maintained for a brief time only may do comparatively small harm. But its continuance is loaded with ever-repeated calamity to the country. In England no man of the smallest eminence comes forward to defend such a currency; its radical and incurable badness is the settled conviction of the English people. Every one would prefer the payment of interest on an increase of the National Debt to the curse of a currency which meant one thing to-day, and another thing to-morrow. In this matter England has nothing to bias her judgment on the one side or the other; such a conviction, therefore, ought to carry weight in the United States.

But how is an inconvertible currency to be got rid of? The answer is not easy—

> "Principius obsta, sero medicina poratur,
> Cum mala per longas invaluere moras."

The roads which lead back to convertibility are many. Each country has its own situation, and the ways of escape are different, though all unfortunately are attended with pain. Man cannot do wrong without in some manner or other having to atone for it by suffering. In England the path of repentance was comparatively easy. The Bank of England was responsible for the notes it circulated, and it was universally trusted. The discount to which its notes had fallen, a guinea being worth twenty-seven shillings in notes, was in no way due to want of credit; the cause was simply excess of issues, which could not, as bank-notes and sovereigns now can, return at once into store. National misfortunes greatly facilitated resumption of specie payments. A large amount of notes issued by county bankers circulated by the side of those of the Bank of England. The war had swollen the price of English corn inordinately; peace brought the farmers of the whole world into competition with those of England. The year 1813 produced a most bountiful harvest, prices fell heavily, and many farmers were ruined. Confidence was destroyed throughout the country, and banks fell into difficulties. In the years 1814, 1815, and 1816, 250 country banks stopped payment, and the quantity of provincial bank-notes was thus vastly reduced. No taint of suspicion came over the notes of the Bank of England; its notes rose in value, and much of the difficulty of resumption was thereby averted. The disposition to demand gold for the notes disappeared, for the notes were as valuable, having ceased to be in excess. Resumption exacted punishment for the past, inasmuch as many contracts to pay or repay pounds compelled the tender either of coin, or of a bank-note as valuable as coin which had become dearer than it was when the contracts were made; but the events here described gradually cleared off old debts and new ones were increasingly based on gold prices. As the value of the Bank of England note rose, it became less profitable to export gold; the bank-note had less the character of an inferior currency, and was less able to drive gold away abroad. Thus the Bank of England was enabled voluntarily to anticipate the day of specie payment fixed by the law and to pay notes in gold in 1821, instead of 1823. No resumption was ever less violent.

Resumption would probably follow the same course in the United States. The important point is to establish a thorough conviction in the minds of the whole people that the return to specie payment is irrevocably decreed. When this feeling has penetrated the entire nation the eyes of all will be turned to the fact that in a brief space of time the paper dollar will possess absolutely equal value with the metallic dollar, and the consequence of this will be a steadily advancing habit of calculating all debts likely to be of long standing, and making all pecuniary arrangements, on the basis of the metallic dollar. Trade with foreign countries will march on the same line, importers will reckon with ever-increasing confidence on a currency as good as metallic. The premium on gold will gradually diminish, and there is reason to believe that the period of resumption will be anticipated as it was in England; and just as the Bank of England found no difficulty, as a matter of fact, in obtaining a sufficient quantity of gold to face any demand for gold on the presentation of bank-notes, so, I believe, will it be in America. But there must be no enlargement of the circulation—not by a fraction—in the meanwhile, for the keystone of the whole building is that the death of the inconvertible paper is decreed past all hope of change.

England possessed an advantage the absence of which may cause some embarrassment to the United States. There is no bank-note paper in America so entirely trusted as the Bank of England note was and is. Hence, Who shall be the issuer of the United States paper currency? becomes an arduous problem. Direct issue by the Government, the Government receiving and holding the sums given by the public for the bank-notes, is a system, I conceive, greatly to be deprecated. It places convertibility at the mercy of political parties. What the Government would do with this vast receipt is not easy to say. Probably it would redeem with it existing debt; but if so, the fund guaranteeing convertibility could hardly be said to exist. In England the Bank is compelled to lodge the fifteen millions in securities. They are a concrete and tangible fund, available always for procuring money—metallic coin. A national debt due by the Government is a very different foundation for the payment of the notes on demand from securities, which can be realised at once in the open market. The want of an actually accumulated fund, and the direct and undoubted dependence of convertibility on a vote of Congress, capable of being passed at any time, would render convertibility extremely precarious. It seems to me—though under the intricate complications which beset American currency, it is not easy for any one who is not an American to speak with confidence—that the best course to adopt would be to imitate the English system, as far as practicable; for that system works admirably in England. As an issue of paper currency it is irreproachable; the only charge brought against it which deserves a moment's notice is that the line is drawn too low at fifteen millions, as the public could and would hold a larger quantity without ever sending any portion of it for payment. That accusation, I venture to believe, has already been disposed of in the preceding pages. To intrust the issue to a single bank under the peremptory condition of investing all that it receives in Government securities would probably be the safest, as it would be the simplest plan; for it might be very difficult to check the issues of many banks, and to acquire a well-founded assurance that the issues never exceeded the amount lodged in securities. On this method a permanent reserve of gold must be provided ; this would obviously be taken from the sum which would otherwise have been placed in securities. A portion of the profits derived from the securities, would of course, as already argued, be appropriated to the State. I do not say that this is the only plan open to the United States, but to the best of my judgment, it seems to be the best.

CHAPTER III.

WHAT IS A BANK?

We have now finished the discussion of currency in its strict and technical sense. We pass on to another agency for carrying on the great work of exchanging wealth, for exchanging goods made to be consumed by men other than the makers—to banking. As currency has no other function than this exchange of wealth, it follows that banking and currency are two different machines for performing the same work. The bank and its great instruments, the cheque and the bill of exchange, transfer the ownership of wealth from one man to another. But banking is not currency, and hopeless confusion must result if it is regarded as currency. Indeed the mixing up of currency with banking, by referring to currency as the cause of many of the most important events in banking, is to this hour the fatal source of the unintelligibleness of that really simple matter, currency. The practice of banking leads to a vast diminution in the use of currency, in the quantity of coin and bank-notes employed; but they are essentially different instruments, precisely as a plough drawn by horses is a different tool from a spade worked by a man, though they both perform the same service of digging up the ground. What, then, is a bank? In what does it deal, for it is a trade? It might appear that these are extremely hard questions to answer, for in what book or speech have they been ever answered in precise and unmistakeable terms? Certainly bankers are not the persons to ask what they deal in, as one might ask the same question of a grocer. Everybody replies—A bank deals in money; people take money to a bank and procure money from a bank—what can be clearer? A banker deals in money as a grocer deals in tea. But is that so? A bank that issues bank-notes beyond doubt so far deals in money, but the issuing of bank-notes is a function superadded to banking; very few banks issue notes. One has only to consider that nearly one hundred millions' worth of banking operations—that goods are bought and paid for through banks to this huge amount in London alone without a single sovereign or a single bank-note being touched—to perceive that money, true money that is handled and counted, is not the staple which a bank deals in, although, like every other business, every bank does touch a small proportion of money. To say that a bank deals in money is one of the most unreal assertions that can be made. It compels the man who gives such an account of banking to call a cheque and a bill money, and if these are money, then farewell to any possibility of understanding what money is. Long ago I stated in *Fraser's Magazine* that probably not more than 1 in 30 of an ordinary banker's receipts consisted of cash, of coin and notes.

This conjecture received a very remarkable confirmation from an analysis made by Sir John Lubbock of a sum of £19,000,000 paid in to his banking firm in the City. It was composed of

Cheques and bills, . .	£18,395,000
Notes, ...	487,000
Coin, ...	118,000
	£19,000,000

3 per cent. only of the receipts were paid in cash, and coin constituted only ½ per cent., or 1 in 200, of the whole sum. Sir John Lubbock's bank has not cash, money, for its staple, for the article it deals in. If that bank does anything, it is not with sovereigns and bank-notes that it does it. It handles some cash, no doubt, but so does every trader and every man in the country. To use money furnishes no indication of a man's business; the cash handled by the cashier of a banker is only his small change; it tells us nothing about Sir John Lubbock's business. If we wish to learn what that is we must look to the big item in his statement, the 97 things which make up the bulk of his receipts. Here we find the commodity in which he trades—bills and cheques—some of which he receives, some he pays. To understand the banker's profession, we must know about bills and cheques, what they are, where he gets them from, what he does with them, how he earns a profit out of them, when they are abundant and when scarce, and what makes them abundant or scarce. Many would say that they are easy to understand, that

they represent money, but I decline to accept the word, represent, in currency, for I cannot understand its meaning there, nor, as experience has taught me, does anyone else; it has no definite meaning for anyone. To say that bills and cheques represent so much money no more tells me what they are than when I hear so many sheep and oxen described as representing so much money, do I learn what sheep and oxen are. Papers which promise or order money to be given, if that is the sense of "representing," cannot be money itself; a promise of a thing does not give it in hand. The thing, the property, is absent. Cheques and bills may do the same general work as money, but so do spoken words, which may purchase goods and bind a man at law just as firmly as the written cheque. What, then, are they? Orders to pay money which can be legally enforced, title-deeds to money which can insist, under peril of a Court of Law, on receiving true money, but which are no more money than those other title-deeds to money which are contained in the accounts of a shopkeeper's books. Cheques and bills say to a banker or merchant—You owe me money; instead of paying it to me, pay it to the man who brings this piece of paper to you. A cheque on a bank implies a debt due by the banker, or a willingness of the banker, when there is no debt, to make a loan of a sum of money; a bill is an admission by the acceptor that he owes money and will pay it on the stipulated day.

These are the things, the 97 out of 100, which a banker receives; they are the articles he deals in. He deals in debts; he receives debts, and his business is to collect payment for them; his customers bring him their claims to collect on their behalf. So far the business of a banker is identical with that of a clerk sent round by a great shopkeeper to collect his bills. The banker touches no money worth mentioning on the side of his receipts; if he handles money, it must be when he gathers up the payments due on these cheques and bills. From his customers—called depositors—he gets only £3 out of £100 in money.

Here arises the question: In what form does the banker obtain payment of these pieces of paper for his customers? If his bank is in the City of London, he will not touch a single pound of money in the collection of these debts. They will all be sent to the Clearing House, where a list is drawn up several times a day of the cheques sent in against and those sent in in favour of each banker who is a member of the Clearing House. A balance is struck for each. Those who have to pay it give a cheque on the Bank of England to those who have to receive it, and the whole affair is settled. If, on the contrary, the banker has his bank in a locality where there is no Clearing House, as at the West End or at Liverpool, then no doubt he must be paid in cash over the counter, but, as we shall see presently, this makes him no more a dealer in money than his fellow banker in the City.

We see then what are a banker's receipts,—an insignificant quantity of cash, and all the rest debts, expressed on paper, which he undertakes to collect. These are his resources—the staple in which he deals,—debts. What does he do with them? which means,—How is it that at the Clearing House he may send in cheques for £100,000, and is paid with a cheque on the Bank of England for perhaps £50? Manifestly, he does not collect money and send it round to each of his customers for whom he undertook to collect it. That would not be banking, it would be a mere collecting agency. The real question is, How comes it to pass that he has a right to receive £100,000 from the Clearing House, and is paid only £50? What are these counter claims against him which have reduced his payment to such a trifle? They are claims of his own making. He knows that he would have a right to receive £100,000 at the Clearing House, but he does not want to receive this sum in money. The money would be useless to him, it would do him no good. Instead of that he finds borrowers, who seek means wherewith to make purchases. He bids them buy the goods they desire and pay for them with cheques drawn upon his bank. The purchases are made, the cheques are sent by the sellers of the goods to the Clearing House against him, they are placed against those he has to receive, and the end of the whole affair is that he carries off a cheque of £50 on the Bank of England.

The nature of banking now stands forth quite clear. A banker is a man who collects debts from one set of persons and employs the proceeds in granting loans to another set. He receives debts from his customers, he creates debts against his borrowers. Thus he deals in debts. Nominally he deals in money, because all these debts are stated in money; but practically and really he deals in money which is due, but not touched, in claims, debts, transferred from one account to another. Hence in my "Lectures on the Principles of Currency," I defined a bank to be an institution for the transfer of debts, and the definition is true. But a still better one can be given, which brings out into clearer light the true nature of a bank, its essential function, and draws away attention from the movements of its machinery, its paper receipts and paper payments with the trifling accompaniment of gold, and fixes it on the realities which generate them. This definition will be derived from the cardinal question, How these debts, which are the receipts and resources of a bank, and those other debts which it creates, are born into the world? For a right apprehension of this vital matter, the exclusive talk about money in connection with banks is most mischievously misleading. People are ever saying of the banks that money is abundant or scarce, money is dear or cheap. This language is freely used by men who are accounted great authorities, yet it is most inaccurate and untrue. It is the unthinking abbreviation, the mere slang of the City. Banking transactions may be enormously increased or diminished without any change in the quantity of money circulating. When banks have much to lend, it is not gold or cash, for that is not the thing lent, but something else which we must try to discover. Again, when money is called cheap or dear, the words express a falsehood, for money (sovereigns) is dear and cheap solely according as the gold of which it is made is cheaper or dearer as a commodity in the metal market. What the City really means is that the borrowing of money is cheap or dear; but a payment given for the loan of a commodity is something utterly different from the cost of the commodity itself. The hire of a hunter for a day's gallop is not the hunter himself.

How then do cheques and bills come into existence? They are the offspring of sales. There are, it is true, many cheques and bills drawn between bank and bank which are not the immediate progeny of sales of goods; but they do not come into consideration here. They are mere distributions among the several banks of a common stock. The origin of that common stock is what we are here concerned with in discovering. These paper documents—every one of them—at their origin denote property bought and paid for, either by the transfer of a debt or a promise to pay later. Every man who gives a cheque to a banker has previously sold something, charged his banker to collect the payment for him, and then he in turn buys and orders the banker to pay for the purchase with that previous cheque he deposited. People who receive their income in cheques or warrants—without sales effected by themselves—fall under the universal law. If their income is derived from a tenant's rent, or a railway dividend, or a dividend on consols—in every case alike, property has been sold to generate the cheques; corn and hay, or a seat in an expensive railway carriage, or goods wherewith to pay taxes, have been sold; there is no exception whatever. The conclusion then is clear; the resources of banks proceed from goods sold, of which they collect the payment. On the other side, the counter-cheques at the Clearing House denote goods bought at some time or other. Further, it is perfectly plain that the power to buy these second goods with the cheques which the banker has authorised his borrower to draw is the consequence of the sale of the first goods, whose seller has received a cheque and deposited it with his banker. Thus the cardinal and final truth comes out, that one set of goods has been exchanged for another — that goods have bought goods — that the banker has acted precisely like a sovereign, has been a tool, an instrument of exchange. He transfers purchasing power, which he received in the form of a debt to collect, and passes it on in the form of a debt he creates. That purchasing power resides in the goods sold, directly or indirectly, by the banker's depositor. It is because the depositor has sold corn that the banker is enabled to authorise the merchant to buy tea.

This process, of course, implies that the man who deposits the debts to collect does not himself buy as much as he has sold, for in that case the banker would have nothing to lend. The counter-cheques at the Clearing House would be those of his own depositor; he could not, in such a case, seek out a borrower and earn a profit on a loan wanted by him. This would not be banking, but only a mere collecting agency. It is because the farmer does not buy to the full value of the corn he has sold that the banker has the means of authorising the merchant to buy tea; in other words, to exchange corn for tea. The cheques given for the corn appear at the Clearing House in favour of the banker; against them there are the cheques drawn by the farmer for what he has himself bought, and the other cheques which the tea-merchant drew on the banker upon the authority given him by the latter. These two sets of cheques drawn against the bank will not equal the cheque paid in to him by the farmer; he will reserve a portion to remain at the bank in cash. Of this more presently.

The nature of banking now stands completely revealed; through its agency corn has been exchanged for tea; that was its function. Each of these articles has passed into different hands; the bank was invented to perform this service. The two substances, corn and tea, and two debts—one due to the farmer, the second due to the banker—constitute the whole affair. Thus we learn that a bank is an intermediate agent, worked, in every case, by two persons, such as the farmer and the tea-merchant, and so, in actual reality, we obtain the definition, a banker is a broker between two principals. In our supposed case one principal is the farmer. He has sold corn, this gives him power to buy. A part of that power he himself exercises by purchasing supplies for his farm; the remainder he does not require to use, say for three months. He might lend this surplus power himself to some borrower who applied to him personally, but he prefers to employ an agent called a banker, and requests him to select the man to whom this purchasing power shall be lent for three months. This the banker undertakes to do, and selects a tea-merchant who wants to buy tea, but has not the means to do so ready at hand. Thus the true lender is the farmer; the banker is his broker, who finds a borrower, and puts him into direct connection with the farmer. The banker is a broker between the two principals, the farmer and the tea-merchant, and the article corresponding to sugar in Mincing Lane, of which the banker is the broker, is purchasing power, lodged in a debt to collect. There need not necessarily be a shilling of money engaged in the whole affair, though many shillings and pounds may have been mentioned in it.

The great value of this definition of banking consists in its bringing out the most characteristic quality of the banker, that he is only an intermediate agent. His sole action is, like a coin, to place property in different hands.

This analysis further teaches us the cardinal truth, that the great events of banking, the abundance or scarcity of its resources, its ability to assist trade, low or high rates of discount, panics and crises, are to be found, not in banks and bankers,)but in the state of the wealth of the country, and in the effects which it produces on the two principals whom the bank has brought together. There is no truth in banking and the money-market more central than this, none that requires to be more deeply impressed on the mind of every trader and every banker. Yet the part which the banker proper plays in banking is vastly important. He it is who selects the men into whose hands the wealth moved by his agency is to be committed. He neither created the wealth which his depositors sold, nor does he touch that other wealth which his borrowers purchase; but it signifies immensely to what sort of borrowers he gives the means of buying, by empowering them to draw cheques upon his bank. On him mainly depends whether the men who acquire the wealth of the nation will employ it wisely, and preserve it by making use of it as capital in processes which reproduce its consumption, or to men who will waste and destroy it in prodigal expenditure, or in unskilful trade, or in reckless speculations in mines, or in making railways in the wilds which cannot for a long period of years reproduce to the country the food, clothing, and materials which their construction consumed. This is the sole range of the banker's action—his selection of the men to whom the country's wealth shall be entrusted; and it is a mighty one. He possesses no capital, though all commercial and monetary literature ascribes capital to bankers. Lines and names in their ledgers, cheques at the Clearing House, debts due to depositors, debts due to the bankers by those who obtained from them loans and discounts, are not wealth nor capital. Incorporeal property is a pure fiction, except as a legal right—that is, a collection of words, spoken or written, which will persuade a Court of Law to order the Sheriff to put goods, substances, into the possession of a particular man. If a title-deed to wealth is the wealth itself, if a mortgage on an estate is the estate itself, then commercial science and Political Economy should be thrown into the waste-basket at once as worthless and time-wasting nonsense.

But, it will be said, when bankers' balances are described as capital, all that is meant is that unemployed capital in the nation, seeking employment, is abundant or scarce. Then why use false and misleading language? Does not Political Economy groan enough already under the load of common words needlessly travestied? Why fix attention on the banks as the actual owners of capital, instead of on their two principals, the farmer and his brother-depositors, and on the causes which may determine them to place a larger or a smaller part of the proceeds of their sales in their banker's hands, and on those who have acquired possession of wealth by the purchasing power lent them by the bankers, whether they are increasing or diminishing the wealth thus put at their disposal? This is a most serious matter; for on it depends whether currency and banking will be ever understood by the world. Those whose ears are filled with this kind of phraseology will rarely be acquainted with the forces of the banking world they live in.

The banker is a broker between two principals, but he differs in one important detail from an ordinary broker. In Mincing Lane the broker finds a buyer for the tea merchant; there his action ends. He charges a commission for the service he has rendered, and withdraws. Not so the banker: he does one thing more, and it leads to extensive consequences. He guarantees the solvency of the borrower whom he finds for the depositor. He chooses the man who shall buy in the stead of the farmer, and does not even declare his name. The deposit of purchasing power passes wholly into his own hands, but on one most serious condition, that he shall return it to the depositor on demand. He has lent means to the tea merchant which belong to the farmer, and the farmer may ask for them back at any time. This fact presents a grave difficulty. It is impossible that a tea merchant, still less a manufacturer, should purchase tea or cotton with funds that he may be required to repay at any moment. On such a condition, banking, so far as it lends means to traders, would be impracticable: a banker would be reduced to the necessity of investing the farmer's purchasing power in buying Exchequer bills, or Government bonds, capable of being resold at any time without any probable loss. But experience teaches him that he is under no such necessity. He discovers that in ordinary times, with a large number of depositors, demands for immediate repayment of deposits are subject to a general law of average on which he may safely rely, and that average falls far short of his receipts. If one depositor suddenly runs his account down very close, other depositors are found to be coming in, without any probability of early cheques for repayment being drawn by them. On this fact, revealed by experience, the banker is entitled to place the same confidence as a Life Assurance Company has to build on tables of the average rate of mortality; and he further establishes an understanding with his depositors that they shall generally leave a fair balance in his hands.

This fluctuation in the cheques drawn upon him by his depositors exposes the banker at all times to pay on a given day more than he receives, and thus compels him to provide a certain amount of cash ready in hand to provide for such a contingency. He is consequently unable to lend all that he receives. He cannot authorise borrowers to draw cheques on him to the full amount of those he has to collect; the difference will reach him in cash; that cash he keeps as a reserve against sudden demands. That reserve furnishes him with protection against the risk of committing an act of insolvency by being unable to obtain back his loans as fast as his depositors demand repayment. It might be, indeed almost always is, a question of time. He has lent on terms more or less long. The bills he has discounted may be perfectly sound, but they are not yet due. He may possess much wealth, but it is not accessible at the moment, or the man to whom he has made a loan may not be ready to repay. Security against this danger, inherent in modern banking, is the object of the reserve.

The magnitude of the reserve, which prudence counsels every banker to provide, is a question of great practical importance. The reserve entails a diminution of the banker's profits; it is coin and banknotes not used, but kept in store; hence, he has a strong motive of interest to make that reserve as small as possible. Still safety is the paramount consideration. How large a reserve then ought a banker to keep? That will vary with the particular circumstances of each bank. A bank in a quiet agricultural district, fed by rich land-owners and steady farmers, whose habits are regular and well-known, will be safe with an exceedingly small reserve. A bank in London or New York, whose depositors are engaged in wide commercial operations, liable to heavy and sudden losses, dealing with distant markets, and are exposed to unexpected contingences, such a bank will require a reserve of much larger dimensions, relatively to the amount of the business which it transacts. Thus there is no fixed rule for the size of a reserve; it is a matter for the intelligence and judgment of each banker. But in every case—and this is the supreme point—safety, protection against being found actually without the cash imperatively demanded by depositors, is the one sole reason for the existence, the one sole law for the management of the reserve. No other reason can be assigned that will bear a moment's consideration. Everything which is urged in support of a reserve, which pleads some other law of the reserve, resolves itself ultimately into the absurdity of the Mercantile Theory, that it is a good thing for a country to import gold into a country for the gold's sake, to be kept like jewels locked up in a wardrobe and never worn, —bought at a large cost, and sentenced to utter uselessness, so far as it is in excess of the demand for small change which society requires, and of the need of reserves of reasonable amount.

In a nation whose trade is spread over the whole world, such as England, and must necessarily encounter the varying circumstances of many countries, bad harvests, wars diminishing industry, foreign commotions striking down the supply of a chief material of industry, such as cotton, trade must fluctuate, and along with trade the funds at the disposal of banks. Thus the equilibrium between receipts and lendings becomes a matter demanding high intelligence and skill from every banker. His reserve must vary, at times enormously. It is natural that he should watch it with a jealous eye. His reserve is composed of gold and notes; and when he finds them diminishing, what more natural than that he should believe that there are too few notes and too little gold in circulation? Give England more gold, cry her bankers, and her reserves will be strong: get more gold and notes into circulation, exclaim trembling merchants in England and America, and bankers will have more to lend us and on cheaper terms. That is, in fact, to say—operate on three parts in a hundred of the resources of banks, and there will be plenty to lend and discount will be easy, even though banking may carry out its transactions, without money, in a single city to the extent of one hundred millions of pounds a week. Such a doctrine is an absurdity on the face of it. Anxious banking and high rates of discount are shown by facts to accompany often large reserves and an expanded circulation. The gold in the bank cannot be lent, and is not lent, the urgent needs of traders notwithstanding. The fact is clear for one who understands the nature of currency. Coin and notes are wanted for those transactions which are effected by their agency; and these are insignificant trifles compared with the transactions carried out by the agency of banking. The transactions in both cases are exchanges of goods; and it is in what is happening to goods, to property, and not in what is happening to the tools that move their ownership, be they metal or cheques, that we must seek for the causes of these anxious times and elevated discount. More gold from Australia, more notes issued, beyond what there is a specific demand for to be used, go into the vaults and tills; they cannot be issued, and are not, whatever may be the pressure in the money market. But this is a fact which banking oracles steadily refuse to perceive. It is perfectly possible—and it has happened over and over again—that a very tight money market with a severe rate of discount, or that an easy money market with a very low rate, should co-exist with the same amount either of circulation or of cash reserve. The gold flowed in or out, as the balance of trade or the payment on debts due by foreign countries required, or as the miners chanced to send it to England in scarcity or abundance; but these same causes may and do go along with pressure or ease in the City.

The important matter for a banker to study is not the movements up or down of his reserve, regarded as isolated facts, but the forces which are acting on that reserve, if he desires to learn the present state and the future prospects of the banking world. It is not the figure at which the reserve stands which will instruct him, but the causes telling on his receipts and his loans. Banking is substantially the conversion of receipts into loans: what his receipts are and are likely to be, what loans he may safely make, and what is his position as to the repayment of loans already made,—this inquiry will disclose to the banker where he stands. When banking effects the exchanges of more than one hundred millions of pounds worth of property in a single week in a single locality by means of loans on paper, it is perfectly idle to affirm that its operations, its danger or safety, its abundance or poverty, turn upon the presence or the absence of a million or two of gold in the vaults of the Bank of England. Granted, if there is a run on the bank from any cause, the presence of a spare million acquires immense importance, as lately happened to the Bank of San Francisco—and I freely admit that to the extent of the gold being actually wanted to face a run, not a word is to be said against the policy of a reserve. To that extent a reserve ought ever to be maintained: it is gold really at work, just as the coin in a shopkeeper's till to give change to his customers. And if the language of City articles, and Economical journals means strictly this—that there is a danger of a run on the bank, and that the bank may come to a stoppage for want of gold—then it is rational and logical, and open to no objection except on the score of the fact observed being otherwise. But that is notoriously what the oracles of the money market do not mean. They mean that the increase or diminution of gold in the Bank of England is and ought to be the regulator of the rate of interest, not because the safety of the Bank is imperilled, and it may have to stop payment—(that is too ridiculous to write, if the Bank's debtors are sound and its property uninjured)—but because of confidence, or the necessity of having some rule, even if it be one of thumb, or any other unscientific and arbitrary reason. The vital matters for a bank are always the state of its depositors and the state of its borrowers. Are deposits likely to increase or fall off, are profits or losses going on in the nation which will act on these deposits, are the bank's loans and advances safe, or have they been granted to persons who have injured or destroyed the property which they bought with them? If the banker's borrowers are good men, still will they repay the loans as fast as his depositors may be drawing cheques on the bank? These are the issues of life or death to a banker, and not whether his reserve is a little stronger or a little weaker. The state of the gold, of itself alone, can give no answer to these questions. The answer must come from the forces acting on the two principals of the banker.

Recently, in June 1875, the money market of London was on the very brink of a real panic. The great Joint Stock Banks of the City discovered that they had made losses that were roughly estimated at half a million, for one of them alone. Soon after the reality of the disorder was disclosed by dividends halved from their usual rates, and by enormous sums set down to the loss account. Was it deficiency of gold at the Bank of England that brought upon these banks such harm and such danger? Quite the contrary—the reserve at the bank was exceptionally high—upwards of ten millions —in a few days it grew to beyond thirteen. The real cause was a banking cause, not the dead uselessness of the idle gold. The disaster lay in bills, in the banking carried on by the bankers in the department entirely under their control—in the lending out of their deposits. They had discounted a large mass of worthless, and, it was alleged, dishonest bills. In other words, their banking had been bad. They had received from depositors a power of buying which they had transferred to unsound borrowers. These borrowers had with this power purchased property, and then wasted or lost it, and could not repay these loans to the banks, when the banks had to repay their depositors. What had gold at the Bank of England, be it much or little, to do with this disturbance, with its cause or its cure? The gold was in large supply—it went on increasing as the ruinous facts were discovered, and the money market was in great terror—interest instead of rising fell—but the banks lost huge sums. They paid away their dividends to their depositors instead of to their shareholders—and so ended the matter. The state of the reserve never came into account at all.

It is hard, no doubt, to investigate so vast a field as

the commercial life of a nation whose transactions cover the whole globe, but on no other tenure is safe banking possible. If the banks of England are acted upon by receipts and withdrawals generated by trading events which may happen in "China or Peru," the bankers must study what is passing abroad in reference to their business, or they must abandon it to mere chance. The gold, by itself, will explain nothing; it will not tell whether they are safe or in danger.

One conclusion to be drawn from these considerations is that the tendency of a reserve to increase or diminish is of far greater importance to study than its actual figures. The anxious question always is how far the diminution will extend, to what lengths the demands of depositors for repayment and the failures of borrowers to meet their engagements will proceed. The object to be discovered is not how much currency is moving about—that may vary exceedingly without having any importance for banking. For instance, the circulation is always much larger in summer than in winter; more is wanted for the harvest and for travelling; but will anyone venture to say that banks are not so safe in summer as in winter, or that this is a reason why the rate of interest should be higher at one period than at the other? Has any sane man ever put his name to such nonsense, however much the fact itself may have been put forward by City articles? The causes which act on banks relate to capital exclusively, to the influences increasing or diminishing wealth. Banking is an agency between lenders and borrowers of wealth.

But this is not the view taken by the City, and those who speak on banking. They set up a different theory, if that can be called theory which is composed of affirmation only; they hold that the amount of the reserve of the Bank of England scientifically ought to, and practically does, govern the rate of discount. Why it should, they do not explain, nor will they ever be able to explain, for there is nothing to connect these two facts together, as cause and effect, but the imagination. There is always a certain mystery as to the future of a vast commerce. When, therefore, the idea has seized upon the minds of men that an outflow from the Bank is leading to a diminution of resources, and morning after morning city articles announce that so much gold has left the Bank, a vague unreasoning alarm springs up which hastens the fulfilment of the disaster it apprehends. Hard times are fancied to be approaching, and lenders take advantage of the feeling, and make difficulties, and exact harder terms—and they obtain them, because the frightened trading public thinks it natural that it should pay more. That the Directors of the Bank of England should deliberately determine at what point the Bank begins to be in real danger of not being able to find gold demanded is conceivable, though I do not believe that for many long years they ever did anything of the kind. But that, when on every conceivable supposition, the limit of danger has long been left behind—when the proportion of reserve to liabilities has reached some preposterously high figures—that in such a case the loss of a million or two of gold, of itself alone, independently of what the cause may be which has generated it, should produce any effect on discount, and justify an increase of the interest demanded, is a hopelessly inexplicable and irrational proposition. It has not the slightest pretension to science or knowledge. It is an easy and profitable belief for bankers; traders are taught to believe that it is a natural law; they are victimised by their own fault, because they do not choose to think and reason.

Let us look at a fact which may teach us much. The tendency of imports to exceed exports in England is most marked and ever increasing. This cannot be the result of ordinary trade, for that is always an exchange of equal goods, though at a particular moment one of the parties may not have given his share, and for the time disturbs the equality by passing into debt, by taking and not giving. The excess of imports manifestly is the consequence of England occupying a permanent position of creditor towards many countries. Loans granted to foreign countries in every form and fortunes owned abroad for which the interest is regularly sent home cause England to receive more than she gives away. Now this excess of imports may assume one of two forms: it may be sent to England in gold or in goods. If it comes in goods the national wealth is increased; there is more to spend as income, or to employ as capital in industry. If it comes in gold, it travels straight to the cellar of the Bank. Is it not obvious to the most uneducated understanding that to import this excess over exports in goods is to make England richer, to import it in gold is absolutely the same thing as to give England nothing, for gold in a vault, if not serving a positively useful purpose, is no better than a heap of pebbles. But it does serve a useful purpose, it may be said, it makes the bank stronger; but what is this but to say that banking is the warehousing of gold and nothing more? The action of human life thinks differently; the imports are sent in goods. England asks for and gets wealth, not machinery for moving it, whether in coin or in banks, whatever those who preach the doctrine that to import gold would cheapen discount, may desire. And do they never perceive that the way to cheapen discount is to increase goods? for as no one borrows of a bank but to buy goods, and no one deposits at a bank but in consequence of his having more goods than he can use and having sold them, a larger stock of goods is an increased supply of the things demanded through banking, and necessarily and inevitably leads to easier terms for lending them.

The reverse happens when there is a diminution of goods, of the national stock of wealth. Thus a bad harvest in England compels heavy purchases of corn in America, and at first is invariably attended by a large export of gold from the Bank. The rate of discount rises. See the consequences of gold diminishing, cries the City, but the cry is the utterance of ignorance. The bad weather has destroyed a large quantity of English capital. The food, clothes, materials, expended on the farming of the year have not been reproduced in corn. That corn must be purchased a second time from the Americans, be paid for twice over with British wealth. The cost of producing the corn which never ripened has been a vast destruction of capital; it was not replaced at the harvest, and consequently those who borrow capital find less in the loan market, and have to pay more to procure it. The departure of the gold, instead of being the cause, is actually a very important diminution of the evil. If the gold were not sent away, the full value of the corn brought would have to be sent away in goods, in capital, and the rate of interest would be still higher. The City may mourn over the loss of the gold and ascribe the pressure to the disappearance of their beloved treasure; they little know that its retention would have added one or two per cent. to the bank-rate in the very teeth of a larger reserve.

The law is universal. Gold cannot be placed in the

reserve of the Bank of England or of any other bank, except at the cost of diminishing the other wealth of the country. A million of additional gold at the Bank means always, and under all circumstances, a million less of other property, of goods, in the country; and consequently an increase of the Bank's reserve is always a distinct loss of wealth and of capital, unless it can be shown that that gold serves a useful purpose which more than compensates for the diminution of wealth. The safety of the Bank is such a useful purpose, and none other can be named, but to say that the Bank is in peril because its reserve is accounted low, or a million or two has gone away, much more a few hundreds of thousands, is senseless talk, unless the probability or even possibility of the Bank coming to a stoppage be shown.

That the power of the Bank to lend need not be crippled by regard for the amount of its reserve was strikingly illustrated by the events of the terrible year, 1866. On May 9 the Bank had a reserve of 13½ millions in round numbers, and had lent 20¾ millions. After the black Friday of May 16, it had lent 31 millions, whilst its reserve stood at 12⅓ millions—more than 1 million less than it had when it lent only 20¾ millions. On May 30 the loans reached the unexampled sum of 33½ millions, yet the reserve had sunk to 11¾ millions. The reserve goes down. In the teeth of this fact the lendings of the Bank rise to a gigantic height. What becomes of the doctrine that it must lend less as the reserve goes down? Did a single man call the Bank unsafe when this disregard for the reserve, and this hardihood in lending, went on? Not one. What then becomes of this miserable doctrine, the great practical rule, that when the Bank loses a few hundreds of thousands, it must contract its operations and make loans difficult and dear? The real indisputable fact revealed by the Bank's weekly reports is that all sorts of reserves accompany all sorts of lendings. Large reserves are found with small discounting, and great advances with small reserves. The man who merely looks at the size of the Bank's reserve will be utterly unable to guess how numerous are its securities, how much it has lent.

But, reply the City theorists, gold rules the rate of interest. When the reserve is full of gold, borrowing is cheap; when gold flows away the rate rises and traders suffer. But is this so? Let us put the question to the same great year of agony, 1866, and compare its answer with those of 1856. In the first week of 1856, with 10½ millions of gold we have a rate of discount of 6 and 7 per cent. In 1866 the gold has mounted up to 13 millions—2½ millions more. At what rate stands discount. At a lower figure, in obedience to the alleged law? Just the reverse. It too has gone up to 8 per cent. On March 21, 1856, the bullion and the rate of discount remain unchanged. In the same week of 1866, the bullion has reached 14½ millions—4 additional millions. Have they told on the bank rate? By no means. They have done nothing at all. It continues at the same figures. On May 9, 1856, the bullion stood at 9¾ millions with a rate of 6 and 7 per cent.; in 1866 there were 3 more millions of gold, and then, as if to mock the City and its doctrine, the rate runs up to 9 per cent. Then comes the return of June 12. There are 18 millions of gold with a rate of 5 per cent. in 1856; in 1866 14½ millions stand side by side with 10 per cent., double the charge imposed on the discount market, in the teeth of 2½ millions more of gold. The statements of the whole year tell the same tale. They demonstrate that the doctrine which makes the rate of discount depend on the quantity of reserve is an absolute untruth—the fallacy of City articles and the practical man. These facts cause no surprise to one who has learnt the nature of currency. He knows that gold and notes are required for ready-money payments only, and that if there is an excess of them it cannot be employed, it cannot be lent, and if it is not a fund available for lending, it cannot exercise any influence on the charge for lending. When the supply for ready-money payments is provided, all the rest of the business of the country is carried out by paper documents, by cheques and bills. But the City may still contend that the Bank can, and, when it chooses, does fix the rate with reference to the movements of the gold. That is true, I believe, it does so occasionally; but the Bank returns here cited prove two things, that they are not obliged to do so, for the Bank gets on perfectly well when it violates this fancy rule, and further that as a fact it does act upon the rule very rarely.

It is no unusual sight to find writers of oracular authority, whether in or out of the Press, in times such as the present, when trade is exceptionally slack and profits are weak, and capital shows little eagerness to embark on new undertakings, and the rate of banking interest is unwontedly low, endeavouring to rally the spirits of desponding traders by announcing that gold is likely to flow in from foreign parts, and will be sure to animate industry, and to improve business, and to swell both wages and profits, and, most of all, restore the gains of the banking world and the money-market. What can be the idea which such persons have of currency? Have they ever said to themselves, in plain words, what currency can and does do? The stock of gold all the world over remains the same, whether the nation is uplifted with swelling prosperity, or whether trade is groaning under biting losses and the money-market convulsed with agony. The only possible thing that can have happened to the gold is to be found in a different place; and will any man venture to assert that gold put in one place in the stead of another —gold which can only have been procured by buying it with an equal quantity of other wealth—makes precisely the difference between the production and the destruction of wealth, between a trade that accumulates riches and one that plunges into ruin? If there be an iota of truth in such a view, let us be told how the gold acts, how it accomplishes these wonders. The mode of operation is essential to the understanding of such effects. Gold, we know, can place goods in one person's hands in the stead of another's; but what increase of wealth, what gain to profits and wages, is there in that, when there is already gold enough for carrying out ready-money payments? There are no believers in magical and mysterious powers comparable to the oracles of the money-market.

But what then is the power which governs the rate of interest? The answer to this question must be sought from the character of a banker, as a broker between two principals. The power to determine the rate of interest at his own caprice does not lie with him, but he is the interpreter for the moment of the forces at work, and he makes a trial of the rate which those forces prescribe. If he errs, events will compel him to alter the rate; in other words, the banker, as the fixer of price in the loan market, is subject, as all dealers in all markets, to the universal law of supply and demand. He deals in purchasing power lodged in his hands by one principal and borrowed by another. When farmers, manufacturers, and merchants are thriving and making profits, they tend to buy less than they receive; hence the banker's means of lending expand. Bad harvests, losing trade, slackening buyers, diminish profits and weaken the banker; there is less to lend. On the other side, opportunities may offer for employing capital with increased advantage, in a colony, in a new industry at home, and the like; the demand for loans increases. Or particular trades may languish, and require less borrowed capital than formerly; loans are in weaker demand, and the rate of interest tends to falling. Or again, borrowers may have lost what was lent them, and their bills are dishonoured, and losses deal blows all round; then swiftly rises the rate. In one word, the events which are happening to his two principals rule the banker's charge for lending.

But these principals of the banking community comprise the whole nation; changes, therefore, which befall the nation act directly on banking. The habits of a population may vary much from year to year. The persevering thrift of Frenchmen steadies the loan market of France; it ever adds to its resources and marvellously retrieves disasters. It is much otherwise with Anglo-Saxons, be they Englishmen, Colonists, or Americans. An increase of property leads at once to an increase of consumption; and that consumption often goes on undiminished after adverse times have set in, thus entailing an inevitable destruction of capital. A fever of speculation will break out, as in the body physical. Because some railways have paid well, and carry large premiums, far more railways are commenced than there are means of completing, whilst the premiums won for their shares are expended in wasteful luxury, to the serious lessening of the country's wealth. There are multitudes of Anglo-Saxons who consume as much in bad years—or other public disorders, such as war—as in good years; the Frenchman betakes himself to retrenchment at once, and then all Europe is surprised, and sometimes uneasy, at the unexpected economical strength he displays. England and America have often made the discovery, to their astonishment, that they have been spending not income but capital; that they not only have not saved when there was nothing to save, but have continued their rate of consumption, and on pay-day, be it for the nation or the individual, have to learn amidst suffering that their property is less than it was. Debts have been contracted, means to meet them have vanished, accounts at banks are reduced, bills are not paid, great firms break, and hurricanes sweep over the bewildered money market.

It is not to be denied that the banker at the moment is the judge of the state of affairs, and may, with or without reflection, determine to lend less or to lend more. But his action is only identical with a seller of cattle at a fair, who, for an hour or two may fix the price of his animals, but, if he must sell them, he must submit to the market price at last.

It must be observed that in seasons of regular trade

and expenditure the actual figure at which the rate of discount stands does not necessarily denote a prosperous or a damaged economical condition. A low rate does not always indicate a thriving trade, nor a high rate distressed commerce. Thus a high rate of interest in the United States and the Colonies implies no disadvantage, nor any exceptional risk; it is a natural result of the great returns which industry gives in new countries; men can afford to pay a higher charge for loans, because capital is so exceedingly productive. Thus some years ago 7 per cent. was obtained for a long period by the Bank of England with ease, and paid with equal ease by the applicants for discount, though at the present time such a rate would be felt oppressive. The superior productiveness of trade at one time compared with another explains the difference of feeling.

But though the law of the banking market places the normal determination of supply and demand in the banking market in the banker's two principals, and in the wealth which they, and not he, handle, it is nevertheless a painful but notorious fact that the banking market is exposed, beyond all others, to desolating storms. The discount market is the most sensitive, the most sudden, and often the most difficult to forecast of all markets. Its peculiar dangerousness in England springs mainly from the vast multitude of transactions, pressing from every region on earth, and converging upon a single centre of commercial credit, London. Often it is very hard to discern in time the forces at work, or to predict their consequences; there are moral forces, too, to be reckoned with, which at times are as fitful as the winds. Confidence enters as an ingredient into banking—confidence in the depositor that the banker will hold his funds in safe keeping, and confidence with respect to the borrower that he will preserve and not destroy what is lent to him. Such confidence is easily shaken when once depositors begin to doubt whether the banker may not have entrusted his funds to people who have lost them. The failure of a few great houses, the explosion of a large finance company or two, the stoppage of a bank is sufficient to throw the banking world into an agony of alarm. Such calamities lie in the very nature of banking, for banking is credit, lending; and the depositor, who knows that the banker will lend his deposit, does not know whom he lends it to. There is plenty of room here for wild impulses of ignorant panic. At such seasons depositors rush in upon the bankers for repayment, the banks urgently reclaim advances, the assistance given to trade, which is the best service that banking renders, and, still more, which is relied upon by merchants and traders as a regular resource of their business, is diminished or refused altogether. Merchants, though substantially solvent, are from this sudden desertion of the bankers, for the moment unable to meet their engagements, and frantic demand for help runs up the rate of interest to a disastrous height. The cause of such tempests undoubtedly resides in the state of the country's wealth; but their violence in the banking market is generated by moral impulses, so well summed up in the fearful word panic. Such crises, as they are called, are inherent in banking operations which cover the whole globe; but the ruin they create is so severe, and their effects, not only on merchants and traders, but on the general population of a country are so painful, that it becomes a matter of high importance to ascertain, as far as is practicable, their true nature, and to seek to gather lessons which may help to mitigate or even avert such calamities.

1. In the first place, a crisis in the money market is something radically different in kind from a disturbance, however severe, in a branch of commerce. From an occurrence of this latter kind the element of vague and reckless terror is absent. This element appears in banking because the depositor has no other security for the safety of his debt but the solvency of the banker; and what wild undertakings may he not have supported with means which belonged to others? The banker, too, becomes very uneasy: what grand houses or companies, whose bills he holds in hundreds, or whose names figure in his books against heavy advances, may be unsound at the core, and suddenly declare themselves insolvent? Many of these houses may be really solvent; but what man can face his liabilities if they are all flung on him together in the middle of apparent sunshine? Then there is always the danger peculiar to banking. If ordinary

persons are asked to pay their debts, and cannot, the process of bringing them into the Bankruptcy Court is long; they are not ruined at once; but a bank that refuses to pay its cheques is instantly arrested in its business; it shuts its doors; and probably will never survive the blow. Its affairs go into liquidation. But the mischief takes a much wider range. If houses have failed in a particular trade, the blow is limited to themselves and the number of persons directly associated with them in that trade. The calamity with a banking crisis is national. Trade in England, to a vast extent, is worked by loans obtained from banks on discount. A sudden rise in the charge for discount, still more the difficulty of obtaining it at all, paralyses trading operations all over the nation which were framed upon reliance on discount and a moderate rate for its aid. The rise to 10 per cent. in a week, or even a day, converts most legitimate mercantile enterprises into loss, or even ruin. In ordinary times business moves along with so much smoothness, that the thought of danger, or even pressure, occurs to no one; yet in these pleasant waters the whirlwind arises with the suddenness and destructiveness of a typhoon. Merchants buy, order cargoes, sign bills, incur liabilities infinitely transcending their own ability to pay, in the unclouded assurance that the bills which they receive for goods sold will be discounted, that is, will be converted into purchasing or paying power by bankers. All traders are mere intermediate machinery between makers and consumers, between growers of cotton in America and the wearers of calico shirts in England. Indeed, trade might be defined as the planting of goods in the places where they are wanted. In performing this function, modern trade avails itself of the resources of banks—that is, to go back to our analysis, the cotton merchant buys by the help of the corn which the farmer has sold. By this process he carries on a business, with advantage to society, far exceeding his own personal means. What if this resource fails him? He relied upon it; but he cannot make bankers prudent. He is no wild speculator himself, he pursues the well-worn path of ordinary business; yet he may be brought to bankruptcy by the imprudent operations of bankers. By the system of bills, the whole body of traders are partners with the banking community, and yet they have neither the knowledge nor the power of checking which real partners possess.

2. In the next place, it is plain that on the side of their receipts bankers are passive; in respect of their advances, the causes which act on banks are mainly of their own making. Deposits are determined by the state of the nation's wealth: a banker cannot make them larger or smaller; but it is his clear duty (and how many bankers are aware of it?) to watch closely the forces which are swelling or diminishing those surpluses of commodities which enable each depositor to sell more than he buys. The banker who desires to be

prepared for a crisis ought to know that the loss of wealth which weakens deposits may arise from two causes: positively, from an actual destruction of wealth; or negatively, from a failure in its ordinary rate of accumulation. One form of this destruction of wealth is full of danger for him, and it is incomparably the most prolific parent of crises; yet it is seldom understood by bankers. Most persons are satisfied if an undertaking is sound in character; if it is no bubble, but a solid investment. They press it forward, and preach to bankers that they are safe, or even patriotic, in promoting such enterprises. Such are works of drainage, railways, docks, canals, and the like. No doubt they are all highly productive of wealth. The growth of a nation largely turns upon the prosecution of such works. But no one stops to reflect that such operations destroy wealth and impoverish until they are capable, not only of yielding profits, but also of replacing what the making of them has consumed. Nothing enriches a country like a well-planned railway; yet the construction of railways is nothing but a gigantic destruction of wealth. A railway is said to have cost ten millions of pounds, and there the mind is apt to stop. But money is no part of its cost; it moved money about, but there was as much money at the end as there was at the beginning of its construction. Its cost is something radically different from money. The making of a railway employed a vast amount of labour. That is, it fed and clothed a vast body of men for a long time; it used up huge quantities of iron and other materials, the making of which consumed food and clothing; and the result is only a line of rails, tunnels and embankments—a mere change in the surface of the land. No one doubts that if the labourers, instead of constructing a railway, had been set to dig holes in the ground and to fill them up again, a flood of poverty would have spread over the country. In what respect, for the time, does a railway differ from such holes? If all this labour had been employed in manufacturing iron and calico, and exchanging it in America for corn and bacon, the wealth of the nation would have suffered no diminution; whilst everything consumed directly and indirectly in constructing a railway, until replaced by goods, by actual commodities, by other wealth, is a dead loss, a real infliction, so far, of poverty. New works of solid and enriching character, but of long replacement of capital consumed, are the very raw material of a crisis.

The distinctive characteristic of a true crisis is that it is the consequences of a previous destruction of wealth. This great feature, in spite of its immense importance for preventive action, scarcely any one notices; yet it is the fact which gives its real significance to a crisis. The expression panic denotes well the agitation which sets in upon the banking world, when losses are discovered and wild suspicion awakened, and general terror is excited, as to who is safe and who not: but the crisis which is the cause of the panic has a far earlier origin. There may be great losses in the money market, many premiums may have turned into discounts, many persons grievously hurt, yet there is not necessarily a panic. What one man loses another man has gained: banking resources need not generally be reduced by the commotion, even though a bank or two may have its credit, or even its existence compromised. The discounting of commercial bills may, on the whole, find lending power undiminished. Again, great losses may occur in a particular trade and yet no crisis spring up. The cotton famine brought heavy disaster on Lancashire, many fortunes passed away, yet at no period of this paralysis of a vast trade did a crisis set in. The calamity came on slowly: bankers, merchants, manufacturers, every one foresaw it, and shaped their conduct accordingly. There was no surprise, no sudden and rapid plunge from prosperity into adversity, no unexpected revelation that men who stood in high repute were undermined and falling, no agony agitating bankers and creditors as to who was able to pay and who not, no hurricane bursting on discount and loans. It is often said in the press that a country has not recovered a monetary crisis for years, but this is inaccurate language. A country cannot be long injured by the mere fact that some banks and mercantile houses have been brought to a stoppage. Gold, notes, banks, commercial firms, are mere machinery: they are not the wealth of a nation. They may fall into disorder, but if that is all, the national wealth remains intact and trade will soon right itself. But it is true nevertheless that the effects of a crisis last for a long time, but that happens—and this is the great truth to remember—because a crisis is only the culminating point of a long-continued destruction of capital which has preceded. Thus in 1825 some thirty millions had been lent to the States of South America, which had left England—as public loans always do—not in money but in goods. The wealth of England was reduced by goods worth that sum of money. Bankers too had largely speculated in mines and other venturesome undertakings, and had encouraged others to speculate. But speculation is not mere betting, for then the country would be none the poorer—the speculation was of a different kind. It set in movement vast applications of labour. Wages were given, which means that food and clothing were consumed: materials were bought with labour—that is again, with the destruction of the things consumed by the makers: the returns made to the capital destroyed were poor, wealth was diminished, banks failed, and losses fell upon depositors. So again in 1847, the potatoe disease had caused a gigantic destruction of wealth. The cotton crop had failed in America, rendering cotton dear, thus diminishing English trade with foreign countries, and impoverishing English consumers. Above all, the construction of railways had been carried on to an extent far exceeding the savings of the country. They could not be completed by those who had committed themselves to the shares. They could not meet the calls. The resources of the banks were crippled. The shareholders had emptied out their accounts, and borrowed, when they could, from the banks instead of bringing in deposits. Shares were unsaleable, except at ruinous loss. But the fact to grasp in all this disorder is that the shareholders had expended their property in setting labourers to work, who consumed the wealth and made diverse constructions on the ground, which did not act as wealth, and were not wealth at all till they proceeded to work in making wealth. In 1857 a similar excess of railway construction had been carried on in America, which compromised much English wealth, and disturbed one of the most important of English trades. France, too, experienced a similar derangement, and then a sharp though short crisis was rapidly developed. In 1866 the civil war in America had overthrown the production of cotton, a crop as truly English as if it had been grown in England. The Americans lost the power of buying English goods. English capital—always in the form of English goods—had been sent to India, to Egypt, and to other regions, to promote the growth of cotton in order to make up the deficiency of the American supply. Houses like the Gurneys had built ships at Millwall and equipped great fleets in Galway with much consumption of wealth: they were not wanted, and were nearly pure waste. Mills and factories had been built far beyond the means of trade to give them employment; the capital consumed by the workmen in building was for the time a dead loss. Abroad towns had been enlarged and beautified with English capital: industries had been opened out in the colonies in countless numbers, whilst at home numerous railway projects had been commenced: the destruction of food and clothing by the workmen was not replaced by unfinished lines: not one shilling's worth of wealth had been produced in return.

So it was in the great American crisis of 1873. Railways had been commenced in the wilds, far beyond the spare capital of the nation to complete. The very process of consuming the capital expended on these works spread a sunshine of seeming prosperity all around. Amidst premiums and unlimited markets for stock and shares all appeared to be growing rich together, and spent—that is, consumed goods—profusely. If a people chose to eat and drink up all their property in one year, gigantic would be the abundance of enjoyments poured out upon every family; but they would starve the next. The time arrived at last, when wealth failed and was not to be procured, railway shares and bonds became unsaleable, and the wasteful but radiant consumption ceased. The national impoverishment then became visible to every eye.

In all these transactions the banks were largely implicated. They did not the less develop the mischief because their securities seemed to protect them. They encouraged new projects, they helped to raise up the premiums, they derived vast profits from the demand for loans with augmented interest. Few bankers dreamt of the specific and formidable danger of a multitude of schemes, however sound in themselves, begun with no other foundation for their completion than a vague reliance on the future resources of bankers. How many bankers knew that they were but mere machines, that the causes of prosperity or adversity lay in the state of the nation's wealth, in the production or destruction of commodities? All goes on thrivingly till at last the means of the nation are crippled by the disproportion between wealth destroyed and wealth reproduced. Then on speeds the storm. The bankers, previously so open-handed, refuse further advances and recall the old ones. Companies are brought to a standstill with works unfinished. Their bonds, thought to be such excellent securities, are unsaleable and unrealisable. Merchants and traders, who have been all along outside of these proceedings, cannot obtain discount except upon ruinous terms. They cannot meet their engagements because the banks they relied on cannot furnish the wonted accommodation. Property is sacrificed by forced sales, and fear and ruin walk over the whole commercial world.

The day of crisis is the day of the settlement of losses, the day of discovering who is to lose. This it is which creates the agony—the panic. The fact stands suddenly revealed that huge losses have been made—that wealth is gone; and then bursts upon a surprised world the terrible anxiety, whose debts are sound and will be paid. The stock of commodities of every kind is found to be fearfully reduced. Those who had the wealth placed in their own hands have used it up and destroyed it, whether by actual waste, or by a consumption unproductive for the time and generating precisely the same effects as waste. On whom does the waste fall? is the question of questions in a crisis. Not on the workmen who laboured on the unfinished railways, for they received wages, and with them consumed the wealth. Nor generally on the contractors who set them to work; they received means to give wages as the work went along. Yet many of these are caught by the storm; it burst suddenly when they were receiving help from banks and financial institutions in reliance on early payments from the real owners of the work done. When contractors fail many are the creditors who suddenly find themselves stripped of their property. Financial houses spread the desolation wider. Countless bills are found to be worthless, and suspensions spring up in crowds. Customers who had contrived to borrow from banks are asked to repay and cannot. Their shares cannot be sold. Banks are exposed to great peril, for their second principals, their borrowers, are failing fast. Still the terrible anxiety is, Who is to lose? for in such a vast machinery of lending and debts, it is hard to tell who are the real owners of the property lost, and must pay for it. If a bank suspends, hundreds, perhaps thousands of persons are brought into danger, nay, possibly into ruin.

In the day of alarm the supreme question is the state of the second principals of bankers, those to whom they have transferred the funds of their depositors. Have the banks lent to men who cannot repay their loans? and this in reality means, Have the banks done good or bad banking? The position of the Bank of England in a crisis affords grand instruction on this vital matter. No one ever distrusts the Bank of England; no depositor suspects that it has lent his deposit, his purchasing power, improperly. Not a man is eager to obtain back his deposit on the ground that the Bank may be in difficulties from its borrowers being unsound. This untarnished credit is the child of good banking. The Bank exercises its specific function well. It chooses its second principals skilfully. No one of its first principals trembles for the safety of the Bank's debt to him. And if bankers chose they might all bank in the same manner, and then the special disaster of a crisis—vague suspicion and terror—would never arise. No banker need lend without solid security. The difficulty might present itself, possibly, that the bank might not be able to realise its loans instantly on the day of trouble; but if the element of suspicion were absent, if the depositors knew for a certainty that they were really safe, the quality of this danger would be very mild. In the worst crisis the tendency of deposits at the Bank of England is not to diminish but to increase. The Bank of England can lend largely in a crisis, precisely because no one is impelled by fright to make a run upon it. If confidence were complete, as here supposed, the Bank might even lend its last farthing, and yet be in no danger. The situation would be known, and its signature, even if its reserve of gold had dwindled down to a trifle, would be accepted by any trader; it would be as good to him as money, the distinguishing characteristic of a panic being absent—distrust. Thus, in the agony of 1866, one of the most eminent banks in London was in some peril, simply because its deposits were immense, and the feeling was not perfect that it had lent with entire safety. No doubt if banks were always to lend with perfect prudence—such as is often seen in agricultural banks, whom the tempest in the money-market seldom even shakes—safety would be procured at the cost of many fairly promising enterprises deriving no help from banks; but security against panics is a benefit of the highest value, and careless banking undoubtedly promotes the diminution of a nation's capital.

It is an invariable sequence of a crisis that the industry of a nation is for a period, more or less long, paralysed.

There is prostration of trading strength. Labourers are thrown out of employment, wages fall, new works are not commenced, or are at a stand-still. Mr Brassey, in his interesting book on "Work and Wages," has described the position of the railway construction industry after crises, its violent recoil from vehement demand for labour and abnormal wages into the depths of paralysis. The ordinary language of the press of all countries on the specific effect of the panic in the money-market is, as before remarked, that it is the consequence of a monetary crisis. This is a complete mistake. The blow which cripples trade and industry is always struck before the panic. As said above, the panic is an agonising inquiry, Who is to lose? on whom is the loss to fall? But the loss invariably has preceded. The banking market is a huge mass of creditors and debtors. The wealth has perished—which creditors are safe? which lose? Which debtors will pay? which not? That is the terror of Lombard Street. There is no destruction of capital in the money market, for it is absolutely destitute of capital. The merchant who got his bill discounted—that was done in the money market—bought corn; what has he done with it? The corn has been eaten. Then what did the eaters reproduce in its place?—anything or nothing? The eating of the corn is wholly outside of the money market; and it is because the corn and other wealth have been destroyed that the banking market is let in for a settlement of losses. One effect, however, it must be freely admitted, the monetary crisis does produce in causing that stoppage of industry which Mr Brassey describes, and it is very instructive to understand it rightly. In such enterprises as railways, town improvements, &c., worked by Joint-Stock Companies, those who take shares command that portion of the nation's wealth which belongs to them to be consumed. Shares are seldom paid for out of income, they are investments of property. Each new call sentences a new portion of wealth to be destroyed for the making of the railway, or any other object of the Company. Now the panic stops this process sharply and decisively. Calls are not paid; the shares are practically unsaleable, which means that other owners of wealth will not take the places of the former shareholders, and continue the destruction of capital. Thus particular enterprises—especially such as Mr Brassey has cognizance of—are brought to a standstill. So far the crisis does throw people out of employment, but it does this because the wealth which carried on the undertaking to the day of stoppage has perished, and there is none other to take its place.

But not only is the disposition of shareholders to invest property brought to an end by the discovery which is called a crisis, but much other expenditure also terminates which was equally a destruction of capital. A prosperous time of such speculation as consists of applying capital to new undertakings, with its premiums and its demand for labour, invariably leads to an increase of expense of living. As already explained, if all England took to eating and drinking up and consuming everything in the land in one year, the abundance and luxury and enjoyment of riches would be what the world had never seen. The same process goes on upon a smaller scale when the speculation which orders the consumption of capital on unproductive undertakings is in full play. Workmen earn higher wages, contractors earn larger profits, dealers in the money market gather up fortunes, and every one spends freely, even lavishly. This spending, this consumption is not of savings, not of wealth, commodities, which were a surplus over and above the ordinary rate of living, but of capital, of wealth appropriated to industry. The day of crisis arrests all this, so that here again the monetary panic acts on the labour markets of every land. But, as before remarked, it is the destruction which preceded the day of panic which renders the loss so long irretrievable.

We thus obtain the explanation of the long depression of trade which follows a crisis. The destruction of capital which yields no return is arrested; the capital lost it takes a very long time to replace, not seldom years. Then succeeds a period of calm, whilst the lessons of the bitter past still live in the public memory. People are shy of entering upon new schemes which consume wealth which cannot be restored for years.

But confidence gradually revives, excitement begins to raise its head again, projects for making new railways, docks, beautifying towns, and the like, reappear, and the decennial law, supposed by Economical philosophers like Mr Mill, verifies itself in a new crisis. It is no law of trade, however, no condition imposed by nature on its machinery, but a law of human feeling. There is no inherent necessity for such recurring periods; they spring from moral forces, and by moral forces they may be annulled. Let bankers learn the lessons which they teach; let them reflect on the nature of the schemes which they support, not their soundness only—for it may be admitted that, as a whole, they do not support unsound projects—but the capacity of the national capital to execute them at the time without temporary disaster. Above all let the promoters of new enterprises study political economy, and learn the meaning of the word savings; they will then know that savings are the excess of goods made above goods consumed, and that it is this excess alone which can, without impoverishment and consequent trouble to the money market, be applied to new undertakings. On the perception of this law, and obedience to what it prescribes, depend the prevention of panics and crises.

But it may be asked—How can one discover whether a nation is devoting to unremunerative enterprises more than the amount of its savings? What banker is up to such a task? It may not be easy; but it is none the less a natural and imperative duty; and it is not impossible. The education of bankers, by study and experience may do much in this matter; the signs of the times may be read, if only the observing faculty and the intelligence to understand are present. More especially must they cease thinking about the reserve of gold being a little greater or a little smaller, or indeed about money, cash, and the state of the circulation. They will never understand the world they live and act in so long as such matters occupy their best attention. The Bank of England sets an example of much judgment in this matter; it is not given to make loans to schemes which must necessarily consume much capital that cannot be quickly replaced. No one has accused it of helping on the construction of new railways in uninhabited regions, or even of new lines carelessly in settled countries; unlike the House of Overends, it does not scatter its resources over half the world. If bankers practised universally banking as good as that of the Bank of England, business would be steadier and disasters less frequent and less ruinous. If, on the contrary, they grasp at every large profit that presents itself, the cause for mischief exists at once, and it will be realised.

But what is to be done when a crisis is on? How is it to be alleviated? The settlement of losses cannot be avoided; they have been incurred, and they must be endured by those upon whom they necessarily fall. But that which is the specific calamity of a crisis, the panic, the suspicion, the alarm and its wild consequences, may undoubtedly be lessened. The great object is to prevent frightened people from rushing to demand payment of their debts from banks and commercial houses, to build up rational confidence when no specific cause for distrust can be shown, to leave banks in possession of resources of supreme value at such an hour for the maintenance of discount to commerce. It must be said, however, that Mr Hubbard declared in the House of Commons, that no firm, capable of giving security, ever failed to get accommodation in a crisis; and let those who are ever talking of the state of the gold think much about this declaration. The greatest force that can be brought to bear at such a moment is an institution like the Bank of England, whose excellent banking bestows on it unassailable credit. Men of banking experience urge the Bank in crises to lend freely; that it does lend thus freely, the enormous loans in 1866, amounting to thirty-three millions, amply testify. But still more is demanded in this direction, and there is some reason for thinking that the requirement is well founded. It is remarkable that in the teeth of a heavy increase of its liabilities there is always a well-defined tendency in crises for deposits to augment at the Bank of England. They are removed from suspected banks, and the suspension of mercantile operations leads traders to place their funds in its keeping for a while. The limit of the Bank's lendings, of course, must ultimately be left to the judgment of its managers; it is for them to estimate the extent to which their depositors may draw upon them. A saviour for them and the money market is always supposed to be in reserve in the suspension of the Bank Charter act; but that has been shown above to be a fallacy.

A practice adopted in the crisis of 1873 in the money market of New York suggests a resource which might be available in England, if necessity should call for something exceptional. The banks associated themselves together, and the association certified cheques—that is, they gave a collective guarantee for the ultimate payment for cheques which they refused in the crisis to pay when presented. Creditors thus obtained complete security against ultimate loss, and an immense amount of vague alarm was calmed down. These certified cheques passed extensively as money—no one doubted their solvency; the holders could use them in effecting payments and purchases. Such a practice could not be directly imitated in London, as the law declares the refusal to pay a cheque to be an act of insolvency, but a variation of form might secure the substance of the relief for the money market of London. The Bank of England might issue certificates, either bearing interest or not, payable at a deferred period more or less long. These certificates would differ from bank-notes in this important peculiarity, that, unlike bank-notes, they could not be returned to the Bank at once and drawn against; they would remain out necessarily in circulation, which bank-notes, as the history of suspensions shows, refuse to do. They would not circulate amongst the general public, but be purely commercial paper. Multitudes of creditors, especially those whose sole motive for claiming payment was suspicion and alarm, would be satisfied with the assurance furnished by these certificates that their claims were safe; they would retire from the frightened crowd that was keeping up the crisis. On the other hand, the Bank would not issue such documents unless perfectly assured of its own safety by the protection of thoroughly sound security. Property is often unsaleable in the day of crisis which a fortnight later recovers all its value. The Bank would escape the danger of sudden demands of its liabilities—for these would have a deferred date of payment stipulated. It would bestow help by means of pledges, which in reality would seldom or never be exacted. It is reasonable to believe that effectual aid against pure alarm and suspicion might be derived from such a proceeding.

But what shall be said of gold? Is not that the resource on which a panic-struck market must ultimately rely for salvation? In the first place, the sole motive for a reserve of gold in banking is the danger of deposits being drawn out faster than the loans granted by the bank return back to its till; and thus it might come to a stoppage, though perfectly sound and solvent. Under this general law the Bank of England falls like every other bank; but does it appear that the Bank in any crisis ever ran a true and real risk of stoppage from the absence of an insufficient reserve of gold? The nearest approach to such a danger occurred in 1825. There was a run on the Bank by depositors. For gold? In no way. The run was to procure the notes of the Bank itself by men who trusted the Bank perfectly, but, in the then knowledge of banking, feared that the Bank would lend those bank-notes to other people, and would not have them ready when these notes were wanted to face the engagements of themselves, the depositors. The Bank was saved from declaring that it had no ready-money by the discovery of a million of unburnt one-pound notes. Evidently then paper sufficed as a reserve—the credit of the Bank was perfect, and that was enough. Mr Bagehot, the advocate of a large reserve, distinctly admits in "Lombard Street" that the panic of 1825 was stopped with notes. This admission, by itself alone—for it was made of the greatest run on the Bank—overthrows his doctrine of the necessity of a large reserve of gold. The same lesson is taught by the oft-repeated reference to the suspensions of the Bank Act. Mr Bagehot incessantly dwells on the assistance received by the Bank from these suspensions. He contends that the Bank would have failed without them. He forgets that the immediate effect of these suspensions, as I have shown, was absolutely *nil.* He forgets too, that in 1825, as he confesses, the Bank did not fail, and there was no gold to help it. But even supposing that these suspensions had saved the Bank, would it have been by pouring into it streams of gold? Just the very contrary. The suspension gave leave to the Bank to issue more paper without gold, and the salvation would have come from the Bank's own notes, its own credit, the willingness of the public to trust it, but not from an additional ounce of gold. Yet the saving power of these suspensions is appealed to by a writer whose one cry is that the Bank ought to pile up a huge reserve of gold. These are crushing proofs that much gold is not needed for the Bank's safety. Nay, when there is gold in the Bank, the crisis cannot draw it out—the gold remains, in the worst of the agony, a reserve, an unused reserve still. It is not lent—plainly because the public does not want it. Borrowers of tens of thousands do not take them out in gold, even in a panic. The Bank's own paper suffices. In 1866, as we have seen, the Bank's loans rose in a fortnight from eighteen to thirty-three millions, yet the gold sank only two millions. But these facts, in the present state of the City's knowledge, do not attract a moment's notice.

These same facts abundantly prove that gold is not the instrument with which panics are healed, and that no argument can be derived even from the time of great alarm for the maintenance of a huge reserve at all times in the Bank of England. But facts and accurate reasoning count for little in the City. "The public," cries Mr Bagehot, "has faith in the Bank contrary to experience and evidence; the English world believes that the Bank of England will not, almost that it cannot fail." What evidence? What experience? The Bank does not fail; that the public sees and accounts evidence. The object of a great reserve, its advocates proclaim, is to inspire confidence in the public. But the public has confidence already, and is not deceived. It had confidence in 1825, though there was no reserve. The public does not require a fine theory about a large reserve; it possesses evidence, fact; it finds that the Bank has reserve in abundance. That reserve has proved sufficient up to this day; it has done its work. It carried the Bank through 1825, 1847, 1857, and 1866; and unless England is invaded, are worse crises than these to be taken as the basis of calculation? A reserve which weathers such storms is indisputably enough. If the Bank had had more gold in those years, could it have lent more to traders, and mitigated the panic? It 1825 all it needed was a larger supply of printed paper. In 1847 and 1866 it had all the gold which the Suspensions set free and could not lend it. In 1857 it lent £800,000 of such gold, but there was a large stock still to spare, unlent, in the liberated Issue Department.

We are thus brought to the ordinary doctrine of the City, that when gold ebbs away discount is bound to be dear, when it flows into the Bank the rate is necessarily easier. Hence the daily movements of gold are carefully recorded: they are held to explain the banking state of the day, and to supply the means of estimating the immediate future of the money market. Accordingly the exchanges are watched with interest; a favourable exchange announces ease; an adverse exchange calls for counter action by raising the rate of discount, and thus tempting foreign money, as it is called, to flow into the country. Great stress is laid on this self-acting contrivance; the writers who expounded its wonder-working power are rewarded with fame. The Bank is pronounced strong when its reserve increases, and this reserve is measured by the proportion which its gold bears to the Bank's liabilities. The whole mercantile world thinks it natural that if half-a-million has left the Bank's cellar, every trader who has a bill to discount should be made to pay a heavier charge, and when half-a-million has come in, the Bank-rate should be lowered. The absurdity of such an artificial rule becomes transparent, in the presence of the fact that the Bank in crises is not saved, nor enabled to lend by gold, nay, that confidence in its stability in such seasons is not affected by the quantity of its bullion.

The marvel is that traders will not learn the nature of banking, and thus save themselves from being victimized. The great events of panics, when they come on, lie outside of the state of the gold. And this being so, what must be thought of a rule which taxes traders according as the metallic treasure is a little larger or a little smaller—a treasure which must be kept locked up in vaults, which does not add a single shilling to the lending power of the Bank, which cannot be, and is not lent, because the public refuses to have or keep this gold unless ready-money transactions have increased. If in the summer travelling expands, and harvest labourers require sovereigns—gold which is sure to return—up ought to mount the Bank-rate, to the profit of the Bank, and to the injury of the whole trade of the kingdom. If the harvest threatens to be bad, and purchases of corn are being made abroad, an export of gold naturally takes place, but the loss of that gold is bewailed in the City; it was bound to remain locked up in the Bank's vault. The object of a reserve, according to the City, is not to be used in the hour of difficulty, but to remain ever buried. The loss to the capital of the nation by the destruction of its harvest, and the necessity of paying with its products for its food twice over does not excite a moment's thought; the gold, the lost gold, the gold which has escaped from its prison, is in every one's mind, and trade must be taxed to recover the fugitive. Is this the language or the thinking of sensible men? Have these persons the faintest conception of what currency is? The City boasts to be a body of practical men—do they ever look at stern, truthful figures? The last pressure of very high discount in England occurred in the autumn of 1873; what do we find in that year? On October 17 a rate of 6 per cent., with a reserve of 35¼ of the liabilities. Three weeks later the same reserve, but a rate 2 per cent. higher. On November 21 the rate rises from 8 to 9 per cent., but in the teeth of the doctrine of the City, the reserve goes up from 34½ to 41½. On November 28 we meet with a reserve of 46⅛, and discount at 6 per cent. But what says the return of January 1874? The same reserve—46 ratio of reserve to liabilities; but the rate of discount, what is it? 3½ per cent. Is it not humiliating to hear men exclaim, day after day, that the money market is easier or harder, because some half-million of gold has come in or gone away, in the presence of figures which show such language to be pure nonsense?

What is the harm, the specific harm, of some three or four millions of gold thus departing to foreign countries for food? The Bank is weaker; but what is the meaning of this word, weak? That the Bank is in danger of not meeting its engagements, of coming to a stoppage? The supposition is too ridiculous to deserve notice. The 33 millions of 1866 crush out this absurdity. A bank is strong or weak according as its banking is good or bad, according as its resources derived from the sale of goods are large or small, and those to whom it has lent have preserved or destroyed the commodities which they purchased with the Bank's loans. What in the world has the escape of three or four millions to America to fetch food for a starving people to do with this banking? There are no bad debts involved in the departure of the gold, no chance of the Bank or the whole banking community losing one penny by the operation. When the foreigners in turn begin to buy commodities with this gold, to replace the corn they sent away, the gold is certain to return. What shadow of a pretext is there in all this to raise the Bank-rate because the gold has left the cellar and set out on its travels?

And if the taking out of the gold for exports proceeded still further, and the requirements of this trade in corn absolutely required an additional supply, what so easy or so unobjectionable as that the Bank should buy gold in some adjoining country? No unsoundness of trade would be existing under the circumstances supposed, no danger of commercial failures or revelations of unsound banking; a particular commodity would, from special causes, be in deficient supply, and the Bank would be required to buy an increase of gold when it could be procured. Well does the *Times* remark, on October 15, 1873, "gold being a commodity which is always obtainable in unlimited quantities and with singular speed by the highest bidder among commercial nations, there can never be such difficulty in attracting it as to cause the slightest inconvenience to any community whose transactions have been based on legitimate credit." What but the terror of ignorance and prejudice could associate the idea of danger, or, as some phrase it, of ignominy, with such an operation? Good banking is the King of the Money-market, banking which lends intelligently and wisely: under its rule, what happens to gold matters nothing, either for danger or for crises.

I may be allowed, I trust, to repeat that which appeared in the *Times* of Nov. 15, 1873: the quotation it commences with shows that even in the City a sense of shame broke out at the deplorable irrationality of City doctrines and practices about gold.

"Sir,—Your City article of to-day contains the following remarkable sentence:

"'That the events which have been witnessed should have actually occurred is a disgrace to the intelligence of all parties concerned.'

"And what has been the cause of this disgrace? One which is implied in the remainder of the sentence—'and this fact becomes still more apparent when it is considered that, but for the service of the electric telegraph in announcing each parcel of gold about to be shipped hither, the panic would have gone on until its mere prolongation might have spread alarm in other quarters and led to serious disasters.' There can be no doubt of the truth of this remark, but is it possible to describe more vividly wilful, self-made calamity and ruin brought on by an artificial cause artificially believed in? The City has trained itself to believe that a quantity of a particular metal called gold, lying in a vault unused and unusable, is the physical cause of the rate of discount, profoundly regardless of the fact, which a reference to the Reports of the Bank of England would at once have pointed out, that all sorts of rates of discount have accompanied and do accompany all sorts of reserves of gold. Instead of studying the state of trade and speculation in other countries as well as in England, its eyes are fixed on the glittering heap, and when it declines the usual consequences of unscientific and purely imaginative beliefs arise, blind terror seizes upon the mind, and men perform deeds which are nothing less than simple suicides. Every man frightens his neighbour: every one sees impossibility to obtain advances hanging over his head, and rushes off forthwith to make himself safe by borrowing from the banks long before he has need of their loans: the banks become shy of lending, and up flies the charge for that discount which is the foundation of modern trade. And what is the parent of all this agony and this disaster? A diminished heap in the Bank's cellar, as if the Bank was going to stop payment, if for a few days it had only half of its accustomed mass—a mass, I repeat, which does nothing for commerce except prevent banking from coming to a stand-still. The movements of gold to or from the Bank may be important as tending to reveal forces which are acting upon trade, just as the foreign exchanges teach us whether England has bought more or less abroad than she has sold. But these movements as merely making the stock of gold in the Bank larger or smaller are not the power which makes discount cheap or dear. If they have this effect it is not from their own intrinsic action, but from the fictitious and absurd significance given to them by unscientific ignorance, and the absence of the ability to analyse facts, which is the basis of all knowledge. That the traders of England should, from utter helplessness of thinking and their consequent surrendering of themselves to all sorts of artificial dogmas, build up by their own act, against themselves, such rates as eight, ten, and twelve per cent., as we have lately seen, is a wonder at which I never cease to marvel.

BONAMY PRICE."

"OXFORD, Nov. 14, 1873."

The convulsion began in September with a reserve in the Bank of £13,238,000, and a rise in the rate of discount from 3 to 4 per cent. It culminated in November, when the reserve had fallen to £8,071,000—and the rate risen to 9 per cent. as the minimum, but when the majority of the loans granted by the bank had exacted a rate actually of 12 per cent. The ratio of reserve to liabilities on September 24th was 44 per cent., on November 5, 36. Upon the doctrine of the City, a reserve of eight millions of stored-up gold, capable of paying off 36 per cent. of what the Bank owed, justified a blistering charge of nominally 9, really of 12 per cent. on the loans taken out by the trade of the nation from banks, and a crisis was averted by the news that gold had been put on board of ships on the other side of the Atlantic Ocean. What kind of conception of the action of currency, and the nature of banking, must those have had who found comfort in this preposterous belief? That corn should fall in price in a famished town when a fleet of corn ships is announced to be in the offing is intelligible; food to eat is at hand: but what can gold do when it comes?

Other causes than the amount of gold at the Bank, we may be quite sure,—causes arising out of the state of the wealth of the nation, out of the destruction of property, and the agonizing uncertainty by whom the loss would have to be borne—generated this violent commotion in the money market: but neither bankers nor traders think of these causes, and one result is the wanton imposition of a heavier charge for discount if some insignificant sum of gold has been withdrawn from the Bank. Thus the attention is called away from wealth itself to the machinery which transfers its ownership, and what constitutes sound and safe banking is made to depend on an empirical, unscientific and false rule.

If the cart only is thought of and not the goods contained in it, people must not be surprised if every kind of charge is made for cartage. What is happening to the two principals of every banker, whether the depositor has much or little remaining of what he has sold compared with what he has bought, and whether the borrower of the purchasing power which the bank derived from the depositor and transferred to him has preserved or consumed the wealth he bought with it, alone contain the secret of the money market, alone explain the events of the banking world.

Hence, as a rule, the banking market is governed by the universal law of supply and demand. Each of these forces may vary, with corresponding results on the price of the article dealt in, purchasing power. Trade may be steady for a long period, with regular movements and uniform growth; the rate of discount at such times will be moderate and little given to fluctuations. Or new and profitable fields for the application of capital, such as the rapid development of colonies, and the demand for capital, may increase much faster than capital itself; a high rate will be the consequence, and it will not be felt to be oppressive. Again, particular trades may have fallen under disturbing influences; a cotton famine may suddenly overtake Lancashire, or commotions in the labour market may interfere grievously with the condition of the iron and coal trades, or costly mining adventures may come to an abrupt end. In such cases, capital will tend to be thrown out of employment; its field of action will be narrowed, and the charge for discount will look downward. Such are the general forces which rule the rate of interest at banks; but trade and its fluctuations, the action of political and social influences on the development of wealth, the likelihood of the increase or the diminution of profits, the probabilities of deposits becoming larger or smaller, in a word the whole field of capital, its employment, and the returns it promises to yield, are matters far too wide and too elaborate for the powers in the money market to study. It is easier, more ready at hand, to look at money, at gold, at the stock of it in banking vaults, at the amount of the circulation moving about the country, at the machinery which moves wealth, instead of wealth itself. Under the influence of such ideas fanciful and arbitrary rates of discount may be ever springing up. It is true these arbitrary dogmas about quantities of circulation, rising or falling reserves, exports or imports of gold, ratios of bullion to liabilities, are everlastingly refuted by the facts of the rate of discounts; but what matters it to bankers? they find a profit in such delusions. But that the great body of traders should tamely consent to be the victims of such empirical assertions, and of such unenquiring, unscientific literature—that they should run as greedily as bankers into these doctrines about gold, never dreaming of looking whether these dicta about gold correspond with fact—that they should be so profoundly averse to study the nature and laws of trade, and be content to accept every kind of quack assertion of monetary oracles about the magical effects of gold being in one place instead of another, to their own infinite perplexity and the grievous injury of their fortunes, is indeed surprising. It is the intellectual mystery of the nineteenth century.—*Populus vult decipi* :—it must take the consequences.

In conclusion I desire to say a few words on the great problem as well as the great duty which lie on the people of the United States. They are suffering from an evil of enormous magnitude, which is entirely of their own creation, and which it lies perfectly within their own power to remove. A permanently inconvertible currency science pronounces to be utterly destitute of justification. The continuance of such an indefensible practice in one of the most important branches of social administration would place that great nation on a level below the intellectual standard which it has won in the world. Were it to go on, their descendants hereafter would speak of the want of intelligence it would imply as the wonderful spot on the great reputation they had inherited. The suffering, moreover, which it inflicts on the people, the wanton corruption of one of the most important instruments of civilisation, the disorder which it thrusts upon all trade, the low level at which it tends to keep the knowledge of political economy throughout the country, the gambling spirit which it introduces into commercial dealings, constitute motives of commanding force which summon the legislature of the United States to wipe away such a disgrace and such a misfortune.

The one vital condition for the successful carrying out of this operation is a genuine and resolute determination of the American people to have a currency worthy of themselves, and to resume specie payments in earnest. Unfortunately it cannot yet be said that this resolution of the national will has been unmistakeably declared. The law orders the resumption of specie payments on the 1st of January 1879; but by providing no machinery for accomplishing its purpose it has rendered further appeal to Congress necessary, and till the measure has finally left the political arena, its success cannot be said to have been secured. It was otherwise with the return to cash payments in England. The Bank of England had been forbidden by Parliament to pay gold for its notes on presentation. The repeal of the prohibition left the Bank subject to its old obligation to pay in specie, which had thus revived. A refusal to give gold for a single note would then have plunged the bank into insolvency. But in the United States the Legislature not only prescribes what the currency shall be, but is itself the issuer of the currency; and if it does not make the necessary regulations to give effect to its own command, there is no law of insolvency which would enable a note holder not paid in metal to seize the property of the American Government.

The renewal of the order to the Secretary of the Treasury to re-commence the contraction of the legal tender issues, which had been regularly begun and then was arrested, is the most obvious and, it would seem, the wisest course to adopt. There is no doubt that the paper issues in America are in excess; the premium which gold bears relatively to paper, or, which is the same thing, the discount and depreciation under which the paper dollars suffer, fully establish the fact. The amount of the excess can be discovered only by actual trial. When the contraction is finally decreed, and its execution commenced, the rise in the value of the paper dollar will gradually reveal that the excess has disappeared. It was so in England; and then the important and gratifying fact was disclosed that the day of resumption decreed by the law could be anticipated, and the Bank gave gold for notes long before it was compelled to do so. There is every reason to believe that the process of resumption would run the same course in America. The certainty that the notes must soon march on equal terms with gold, and the steady effects of the continuous contraction, would make men feel in all the markets before the actual day of positive fact arrived, that the paper and the metallic dollar were the same things.

Many apprehend that contraction would create a

deficiency of currency to the consequent injury of trade; but this is an entire mistake. If by contraction is meant that there would be too little currency with gold and notes convertible into gold to do the work of cash payments, of carrying out that buying and selling which is effected by ready money, then such contraction would cause inconvenience; but such a state of things could not arise if notes were always to be procured from the issuers subject to the obligation of redemption in specie if demanded. This was before 1844 the state of currency in England; and assuredly no one complained in those times that currency was inconveniently scarce.

Moreover, as I have shown above, a deficiency of a particular tool of exchange is always of slight duration, and is easily remedied in many ways. Smaller cheques would spring up in abundance, banking machinery be more used, and credit, for a while, in small matters enlarged. The greatest inconvenience from such a deficiency to society would be a real scarcity of shillings and pence as occurred occasionally in England; were it to last any time, very small notes would speedily make their appearance. The United States would be protected by their small notes.

The true inconvenience resulting from contraction lies in a totally different region, and would undoubtedly be real, and must be fairly admitted. We have seen that an inconvertible paper currency leads to a rise of general prices in all markets. The notes are worth less than metallic dollars, they are depreciated; every seller in every store is obliged to demand more of them for the same goods, in order to obtain in the paper money the full value of the things he sells. Under contraction the difference between gold and paper would lessen and ultimately disappear; and along with this movement there would be another by its side in prices which would gradually become less. The effect of this process on debtors and creditors would be real. Every debtor who owed paper dollars would find, as contraction went on, that to procure these notes he must give a larger quantity of his property. He is pledged to pay so many dollars; but as the dollars grew in value, the prices of his goods would be lower, because each single dollar was worth more, and to procure the dollars necessary to discharge his debt, he cannot acquire them except at a larger cost of property given for them. Thus, as the paper dollar advances to par with gold, the debtor whose debt is of long standing necessarily loses. But equally did the creditors lose as inflation went on; they successively received dollars which bought less and less as prices advanced in the stores. This inevitable loss to debtors and creditors in turn is the curse of inconvertible currency, and for that very reason it is that steadiness of value is the first quality of a good currency. The loss which resumption will bring to some debtors is to be regretted, but it cannot in any way be pleaded as a ground for persevering in inconvertible notes and rejecting specie payments. In the first place, this loss will go on, and does go on now, incessantly, and the premium on gold varies constantly from time to time; it has varied from upwards of 133 to 10, between 1865 and 1871—and all these movements up and down have injured debtors or creditors. This fact alone suffices to repel the objection that contraction and resumption will injure debtors. But secondly, with a period so distant as 1879, most old debts will have been cleared off, and all new ones be made more and more on the basis of a dollar of gold. The ultimate remainder of old debts, formed under a great difference between paper and gold, would be insignificant.

But even were it not so, and that a serious loss must fall on debtors, the plea that this loss ought to bar the resumption of specie payment would deserve no consideration whatever. It proves too much, and that fault in logic renders every argument worthless. It would land mankind in a practical absurdity of the highest order. To demand that bad legislation shall be persevered in because the return to good legislation would involve suffering to some, or even to all, would sentence society to moral petrifaction. Progress would be impossible, for the mode of existence of man would have been surrendered to a past generation which had made bad laws that could not be altered. Men, whether as collected in nations or as individuals, cannot do wrong without suffering, and that suffering must be endured, if the wrong is to be made to cease. It is pure irrationality, and never is or could be endured in practice, that a nation cannot put away evil because some pain must be incurred in the act. How many keepers of hotels and owners of coaches were deeply injured in England by the introduction of railways? How many in the United States by the abolition of slavery? The loss which a few debtors would suffer by resumption cannot be taken into the least account against the abolition of so bad and loss-inflicting an institution as an inconvertible paper currency. Whether that loss could be mitigated by some arrangements in the carrying out of resumption is a totally different matter, and one quite deserving of consideration; but I confess I have seen no suggestion respecting it which seems practicable, and I am not aware that any country, on its return back to metallic currency, adopted any process of this nature.

APPENDIX.

It seems desirable to add the following remarks to Chapter I.:—

A.

THIS option of the debtor to select that currency whose metallic value is overrated by the law of legal tender illustrates the principle that a better currency is always driven off by one that is inferior. Thus when some little time ago silver in France possessed a higher value than that assigned to it by the relation of twenty francs being equal to one Napoleon, it became profitable to purchase silver francs with imported gold, which was converted into Napoleons or accepted in payment as being equivalent to twenty francs. This profit poured an immense quantity of gold into France, and the old premium which travellers had to pay on entering France to obtain gold coins vanished, and the currency of France was to a large degree converted into gold. Silver left her shores; for there was gain in buying silver coins with imported gold, to sell later the purchased silver at its natural value in some foreign land. Similarly with light sovereigns in England, they pass from hand to hand undetected, each holder of them assuming them to be of full weight, and each one preferring the chance of being able to pass them on to the trouble of weighing them before accepting them in payment. But there are a few who know better, and whose continuous action has great results. They are under the obligation to remit gold to foreign countries, and they are careful to select the sovereigns of full weight. The light ones remain in England, ever increased in number by the wear and tear of daily use, and it is not difficult to foresee that they might constitute so large a proportion of the metallic currency of the nation as to call for a rectification of their deficient value at the cost of the last unfortunate holders.

Adulterated coins stand on a rather different basis. They are not light coins, reduced in weight by wear and tear. They are full-weighted of their kind, but the quantity of precious metal contained in them is intentionally reduced below the amount credited to them by popular belief. The mediæval kings who issued them gave less silver or gold in paying their debts with them than their creditors were entitled to receive upon the authorised understanding of the weight and fineness which ought to be contained in them. This was, of course, a palpable fraud in the payment of debts. But it is important to remark that, unlike light coins, they were sound money to the extent of the gold or silver of which they were composed. If a quarter of a sovereign in gold had been suppressed in the coining of it, the deficiency of weight being made up with inferior metal, it would still be a good coin for fifteen shillings, as good as the unadulterated one was for twenty. Every foreign exchange would be altered; the sovereign being estimated in every foreign currency as a coin worth fifteen shillings' worth of gold, the exchange would fall by one quarter. The fraud of the issue would have been perpetrated once for all: the plundered creditor would receive three-fourths only of what was his due; but, nevertheless, he would have had a good fifteen shillings coin. Such an adulteration is now impossible, but it is well to understand correctly the real character of what was done in the past.

B.

Extract from Professor Perry's Address at Omaha, October 1, 1874.

Why worse for farmers.—An inconvertible paper money always depreciated and always variable is worse for farmers than for almost anybody else; first, on the ground of its depreciation; and second, on the ground of its variability. As the value of money goes down, of course general prices tend to rise; but, unfortunately, they do not rise equally, nor in equal times; and some prices do not rise at all. For example, manufactured goods are quickest to experience a rise of price owing to a depreciation of the currency, because as a rule manufacturers are intelligent men and know the tendency of depreciated money to depreciate more, and thus hasten to insure themselves by putting a higher price on their goods. Wages rise much more slowly than goods, and never proportionably, because labourers do not well understand the situation, and never act quickly enough to ensure themselves; and so they are always great sufferers from a depreciated money. Real estate rises slowly and irregularly, though at times tumultuously, under such money, and never on the average so high as manufactured goods rise; while agricultural products, some parts of which are exported to foreign countries, scarcely rise in price at all. The reason for this is, that the foreign gold price of that part which is exported largely determines the home price of the whole crop. There is only one wholesale price of wheat of the same grade in New York city, whether it is for export or whether it is for home consumption. The gold price in Liverpool determines the currency price in New York just so long as any wheat is exported; and the price in New York determines the price in Chicago and Omaha. If the premium on gold, in consequence of the use of a depreciated currency, were as high as the average rise of prices arising from that depreciation, it would not be so unjust; but it never is. Gold is generally the cheapest thing a-going, so soon as an inferior currency has demonetised it and thrown it out of demand; and the whole consequence to farmers of the use of such a poor money is, that they have to pay a great deal more for all that they need to buy, and only get a very little more or nothing at all for all that they have to sell. Wheat was no higher in currency in 1873 than it was in gold in 1860; hams were not; lard was not; and salt pork was not. These are all exportable agricultural products whose current price is determined by the gold money of the world's great market. These things are what farmers *sell*. But harnesses, boots and shoes, hats and caps, blankets, all manner of clothing, were much higher in 1873 than they were in 1860. These manufactures are what farmers have to *buy*.

The injustice of it.—The mischief of paper money is, that it affects different classes differently, and the largest class the most injuriously of all. It raises some prices much, other prices little, and still other prices not at all. Some prices are raised quickly and pretty regularly, and other prices are raised slowly and irregularly; so that the shrewd ones always take advantage of the ignorant ones, and the dishonest ones of the honest ones. The whole trick of the thing is a trick of distribution. Some men may get rich out of it, but this is always at the expense of other men. All classes of the people are ultimately great losers in wealth and reputation from the destruction of the stable measure of value—from disturbing the meaning of the word dollar. A huge crop of defaulters and of failures and of bursted speculations and of ruined reputations are always the harvest of that sowing. But farmers always have been and always will be the greatest losers from rag-money; partly for the reason that I have just given—namely, that what they have to buy is enhanced in price by it, while what they have to sell is not enhanced in price by it; and partly also, because it takes the farmer almost a year to realise on his crops, and he cannot meanwhile insure himself against the inevitable changes in the currency. The dollar in which he calculates the *expenses* of his crop is almost sure not to be the dollar in which he realises the *results* of his crops. He cannot calculate. He cannot insure himself. He is helpless. The manufacturer who turns off his product weekly or monthly can vary his prices weekly or monthly, and save himself at least in part; but the farmer, poor man, can do no such thing. He is at the mercy of currency-tinkers. Because all our paper money is only a promise to pay, and an unfulfilled promise at that; because it is depreciated far below the solid money of the world's market; because it is variable in value from day to day and from year to year, unsettling the measure of all other values; because such money always stimulates speculation and hampers productive industry; because it corrupts public morals, undermines honesty, and makes defaulters, by destroying the stable standard of value; because it unjustly distributes the rewards of industry, and cheats by wholesale the whole farming interests; and because such money has always been followed by these results wheresoever the experiment has been tried; I do hereby invite all farmers, east and west, all grangers, north and south, and all other true men, to unite with me in raising a cry that shall pierce the dulled ears of our rulers—AN HONEST CRY FOR AN HONEST DOLLAR.

THE INTERNATIONAL SCIENTIFIC SERIES.

FORTHCOMING VOLUMES.

Prof. H. SAINTE-CLAIRE DEVILLE. *An Introduction to General Chemistry.*

Prof. WURTZ. *Atoms and the Atomic Theory.*

Prof. De QUATREFAGES. *The Human Race.*

Prof. LACAZE-DUTHIERS. *Zoölogy since Cuvier.*

Prof. BERTHELOT. *Chemical Synthesis.*

Prof. C. A. YOUNG, Ph. D. (of Dartmouth College). *The Sun.*

Prof. OGDEN N. ROOD (Columbia College, N. Y.). *Modern Chromatics and its Relations to Art and Industry.*

Dr. EUGENE LOMMEL (University of Erlangen). *The Nature of Light.*

Prof. J. ROSENTHAL. *General Physiology of Muscles and Nerves.*

Prof. JAMES D. DANA, M. A., LL. D. *On Cephalization; or, Head-characters in the Gradation and Progress of Life.*

Prof. S. W. JOHNSON, M. A. *On the Nutrition of Plants.*

Prof. AUSTIN FLINT, Jr., M. D. *The Nervous System, and its Relation to the Bodily Functions.*

Prof. BERNSTEIN (University of Halle). *The Five Senses of Man.*

Prof. FERDINAND COHN (Breslau University). *Thallophytes (Algæ, Lichens Fungi).*

Prof. HERMANN (University of Zurich). *Respiration.*

Prof. LEUCKART (University of Leipsic). *Outlines of Animal Organization.*

Prof. LIEBREICH (University of Berlin). *Outlines of Toxicology.*

Prof. KUNDT (University of Strasburg). *On Sound.*

Prof. REES (University of Erlangen). *On Parasitic Plants.*

Prof. STEINTHAL (University of Berlin). *Outlines of the Science of Language.*

P. BERT (Professor of Physiology, Paris). *Forms of Life and other Cosmical Conditions.*

E. ALGLAVE (Professor of Constitutional and Administrative Law at Douai, and of Political Economy at Lille). *The Primitive Elements of Political Constitutions.*

P. LORAIN (Professor of Medicine, Paris). *Modern Epidemics.*

Prof. SCHUTZENBERGER (Director of the Chemical Laboratory at the Sorbonne). *On Fermentations.*

Mons. FREIDEL. *The Functions of Organic Chemistry.*

Mons. DEBRAY. *Precious Metals.*

Prof. CORFIELD, M. A., M. D. (Oxon.). *Air in its Relation to Health.*

Prof. A. GIARD. *General Embryology.*

D. APPLETON & CO., PUBLISHERS, 549 & 551 Broadway, N. Y.

III.

Foods.

By Dr. EDWARD SMITH.

1 vol., 12mo. Cloth. Illustrated. . . . . Price, $1.75.

In making up THE INTERNATIONAL SCIENTIFIC SERIES, Dr. Edward Smith was selected as the ablest man in England to treat the important subject of Foods. His services were secured for the undertaking, and the little treatise he has produced shows that the choice of a writer on this subject was most fortunate, as the book is unquestionably the clearest and best-digested compend of the Science of Foods that has appeared in our language.

"The book contains a series of diagrams, displaying the effects of sleep and meals on pulsation and respiration, and of various kinds of food on respiration, which, as the results of Dr. Smith's own experiments, possess a very high value. We have not far to go in this work for occasions of favorable criticism; they occur throughout, but are perhaps most apparent in those parts of the subject with which Dr. Smith's name is especially linked."—*London Examiner.*

"The union of scientific and popular treatment in the composition of this work will afford an attraction to many readers who would have been indifferent to purely theoretical details. . . . Still his work abounds in information, much of which is of great value, and a part of which could not easily be obtained from other sources. Its interest is decidedly enhanced for students who demand both clearness and exactness of statement, by the profusion of well-executed woodcuts, diagrams, and tables, which accompany the volume. . . . The suggestions of the author on the use of tea and coffee, and of the various forms of alcohol, although perhaps not strictly of a novel character, are highly instructive, and form an interesting portion of the volume."—*N. Y. Tribune.*

IV.

Body and Mind.

THE THEORIES OF THEIR RELATION.

By ALEXANDER BAIN, LL. D.

1 vol., 12mo. Cloth. . . . . Price, $1.50.

PROFESSOR BAIN is the author of two well-known standard works upon the Science of Mind—"The Senses and the Intellect," and "The Emotions and the Will." He is one of the highest living authorities in the school which holds that there can be no sound or valid psychology unless the mind and the body are studied, as they exist, together.

"It contains a forcible statement of the connection between mind and body, studying their subtile interworkings by the light of the most recent physiological investigations. The summary in Chapter V., of the investigations of Dr. Lionel Beale of the embodiment of the intellectual functions in the cerebral system, will be found the freshest and most interesting part of his book. Prof. Bain's own theory of the connection between the mental and the bodily part in man is stated by himself to be as follows: There is 'one substance, with two sets of properties, two sides, the physical and the mental—a *double-faced unity.*' While, in the strongest manner, asserting the union of mind with brain, he yet denies 'the association of union *in place,*' but asserts the union of close succession in time,' holding that 'the same being is, by alternate fits, under extended and under unextended consciousness.'"—*Christian Register.*

V.

The Study of Sociology.

By HERBERT SPENCER.

1 vol., 12mo. Cloth. . . . . Price, $1.50.

"The philosopher whose distinguished name gives weight and influence to this volume, has given in its pages some of the finest specimens of reasoning in all its forms and departments. There is a fascination in his array of facts, incidents, and opinions, which draws on the reader to ascertain his conclusions. The coolness and calmness of his treatment of acknowledged difficulties and grave objections to his theories win for him a close attention and sustained effort, on the part of the reader, to comprehend, follow, grasp, and appropriate his principles. This book, independently of its bearing upon sociology, is valuable as lucidly showing what those essential characteristics are which entitle any arrangement and connection of facts and deductions to be called a *science*."—*Episcopalian.*

"This work compels admiration by the evidence which it gives of immense research, study, and observation, and is, withal, written in a popular and very pleasing style. It is a fascinating work, as well as one of deep practical thought."—*Bost. Post.*

"Herbert Spencer is unquestionably the foremost living thinker in the psychological and sociological fields, and this volume is an important contribution to the science of which it treats. . . . It will prove more popular than any of its author's other creations, for it is more plainly addressed to the people and has a more practical and less speculative cast. It will require thought, but it is well worth thinking about."—*Albany Evening Journal.*

VI.

The New Chemistry.

By JOSIAH P. COOKE, Jr.,

Erving Professor of Chemistry and Mineralogy in Harvard University.

1 vol., 12mo. Cloth. . . . . Price, $2.00.

"The book of Prof. Cooke is a model of the modern popular science work. It has just the due proportion of fact, philosophy, and true romance, to make it a fascinating companion, either for the voyage or the study."—*Daily Graphic.*

"This admirable monograph, by the distinguished Erving Professor of Chemistry in Harvard University, is the first American contribution to 'The International Scientific Series,' and a more attractive piece of work in the way of popular exposition upon a difficult subject has not appeared in a long time. It not only well sustains the character of the volumes with which it is associated, but its reproduction in European countries will be an honor to American science."—*New York Tribune.*

"All the chemists in the country will enjoy its perusal, and many will seize upon it as a thing longed for. For, to those advanced students who have kept well abreast of the chemical tide, it offers a calm philosophy. To those others, youngest of the class, who have emerged from the schools since new methods have prevailed, it presents a generalization, drawing to its use all the data, the relations of which the newly-fledged fact-seeker may but dimly perceive without its aid. . . . To the old chemists, Prof. Cooke's treatise is like a message from beyond the mountain. They have heard of changes in the science; the clash of the battle of old and new theories has stirred them from afar. The tidings, too, had come that the old had given way; and little more than this they knew. . . . Prof. Cooke's 'New Chemistry' must do wide service in bringing to close sight the little known and the longed for. . . . As a philosophy it is elementary, but, as a book of science, ordinary readers will find it sufficiently advanced."—*Utica Morning Herald.*

VII.

The Conservation of Energy.

By BALFOUR STEWART, LL. D., F. R. S.

With an Appendix treating of the Vital and Mental Applications of the Doctrine.

1 vol., 12mo. Cloth. Price, $1.50.

"The author has succeeded in presenting the facts in a clear and satisfactory manner, using simple language and copious illustration in the presentation of facts and principles, confining himself, however, to the physical aspect of the subject. In the Appendix the operation of the principles in the spheres of life and mind is supplied by the essays of Professors Le Conte and Bain."—*Ohio Farmer.*

"Prof. Stewart is one of the best known teachers in Owens College in Manchester. "The volume of THE INTERNATIONAL SCIENTIFIC SERIES now before us is an excellent illustration of the true method of teaching, and will well compare with Prof. Tyndall's charming little book in the same series on 'Forms of Water," with illustrations enough to make clear, but not to conceal his thoughts, in a style simple and brief."—*Christian Register, Boston.*

"The writer has wonderful ability to compress much information into a few words. It is a rich treat to read such a book as this, when there is so much beauty and force combined with such simplicity.—*Eastern Press.*

VIII.

Animal Locomotion;

Or, WALKING, SWIMMING, AND FLYING.

With a Dissertation on Aëronautics.

By J. BELL PETTIGREW, M. D., F. R. S., F. R. S. E., F. R. C. P. E.

1 vol., 12mo. . . . . . Price, $1.75.

"This work is more than a contribution to the stock of entertaining knowledge, though, if it only pleased, that would be sufficient excuse for its publication. But Dr. Pettigrew has given his time to these investigations with the ultimate purpose of solving the difficult problem of Aëronautics. To this he devotes the last fifty pages of his book. Dr. Pettigrew is confident that man will yet conquer the domain of the air."—*N. Y. Journal of Commerce.*

"Most persons claim to know how to walk, but few could explain the mechanical principles involved in this most ordinary transaction, and will be surprised that the movements of bipeds and quadrupeds, the darting and rushing motion of fish, and the erratic flight of the denizens of the air, are not only anologous, but can be reduced to similar formula. The work is profusely illustrated, and, without reference to the theory it is designed to expound, will be regarded as a valuable addition to natural history." —*Omaha Republic.*

D. APPLETON & CO., PUBLISHERS, 549 & 551 Broadway, N. Y.

IX.

Responsibility in Mental Disease.

By HENRY MAUDSLEY, M. D.,

Fellow of the Royal College of Physicians; Professor of Medical Jurisprudence in University College, London.

1 vol., 12mo. Cloth. . . Price, $1.50.

"Having lectured in a medical college on Mental Disease, this book has been a feast to us. It handles a great subject in a masterly manner, and, in our judgment, the positions taken by the author are correct and well sustained."—*Pastor and People.*

"The author is at home in his subject, and presents his views in an almost singularly clear and satisfactory manner. . . . The volume is a valuable contribution to one of the most difficult, and at the same time one of the most important subjects of investigation at the present day."—*N. Y. Observer.*

"It is a work profound and searching, and abounds in wisdom."—*Pittsburg Commercial.*

"Handles the important topic with masterly power, and its suggestions are practical and of great value."—*Providence Press.*

X.

The Science of Law.

By SHELDON AMOS, M.A.,

Professor of Jurisprudence in University College, London; author of "A Systematic View of the Science of Jurisprudence," "An English Code, its Difficulties and the Modes of overcoming them," etc., etc.

1 vol., 12mo. Cloth. . . . . Price, $1.75.

"The valuable series of 'International Scientific' works, prepared by eminent specialists, with the intention of popularizing information in their several branches of knowledge, has received a good accession in this compact and thoughtful volume. It is a difficult task to give the outlines of a complete theory of law in a portable volume, which he who runs may read, and probably Professor Amos himself would be the last to claim that he has perfectly succeeded in doing this. But he has certainly done much to clear the science of law from the technical obscurities which darken it to minds which have had no legal training, and to make clear to his 'lay' readers in how true and high a sense it can assert its right to be considered a science, and not a mere practice."—*The Christian Register.*

"The works of Bentham and Austin are abstruse and philosophical, and Maine's require hard study and a certain amount of special training. The writers also pursue different lines of investigation, and can only be regarded as comprehensive in the departments they confined themselves to. It was left to Amos to gather up the result and present the science in its fullness. The unquestionable merits of this, his last book, are, that it contains a complete treatment of a subject which has hitherto been handled by specialists, and it opens up that subject to every inquiring mind. . . . To do justice to 'The Science of Law' would require a longer review than we have space for. We have read no more interesting and instructive book for some time. Its themes concern every one who renders obedience to laws, and who would have those laws the best possible. The tide of legal reform which set in fifty years ago has to sweep yet higher if the flaws in our jurisprudence are to be removed. The process of change cannot be better guided than by a well-informed public mind, and Prof. Amos has done great service in materially helping to promote this end."—*Buffalo Courier.*

XI.

Animal Mechanism,

A Treatise on Terrestrial and Aërial Locomotion.

By E. J. MAREY,

Professor at the College of France, and Member of the Academy of Medicine.

With 117 Illustrations, drawn and engraved under the direction of the author.

1 vol., 12mo. Cloth. . . . . Price, $1.75

"We hope that, in the short glance which we have taken of some of the most important points discussed in the work before us, we have succeeded in interesting our readers sufficiently in its contents to make them curious to learn more of its subject-matter. We cordially recommend it to their attention.

"The author of the present work, it is well known, stands at the head of those physiologists who have investigated the mechanism of animal dynamics—indeed, we may almost say that he has made the subject his own. By the originality of his conceptions, the ingenuity of his constructions, the skill of his analysis, and the perseverance of his investigations, he has surpassed all others in the power of unveiling the complex and intricate movements of animated beings."—*Popular Science Monthly.*

XII.

History of the Conflict between Religion and Science.

By JOHN WILLIAM DRAPER, M. D., LL. D.,

Author of "The Intellectual Development of Europe."

1 vol., 12mo. . . . . Price, $1.75.

"This little 'History' would have been a valuable contribution to literature at any time, and is, in fact, an admirable text-book upon a subject that is at present engrossing the attention of a large number of the most serious-minded people, and it is no small compliment to the sagacity of its distinguished author that he has so well gauged the requirements of the times, and so adequately met them by the preparation of this volume. It remains to be added that, while the writer has flinched from no responsibility in his statements, and has written with entire fidelity to the demands of truth and justice, there is not a word in his book that can give offense to candid and fair-minded readers."—*N. Y. Evening Post.*

"The key-note to this volume is found in the antagonism between the progressive tendencies of the human mind and the pretensions of ecclesiastical authority, as developed in the history of modern science. No previous writer has treated the subject from this point of view, and the present monograph will be found to possess no less originality of conception than vigor of reasoning and wealth of erudition. . . . The method of Dr. Draper, in his treatment of the various questions that come up for discussion, is marked by singular impartiality as well as consummate ability. Throughout his work he maintains the position of an historian, not of an advocate. His tone is tranquil and serene, as becomes the search after truth, with no trace of the impassioned ardor of controversy. He endeavors so far to identify himself with the contending parties as to gain a clear comprehension of their motives, but, at the same time, he submits their actions to the tests of a cool and impartial examination."—*N. Y. Tribune.*

XIII.

THE DOCTRINE OF

Descent, and Darwinism.

By OSCAR SCHMIDT,

Professor in the University of Strasburg.

WITH 26 WOODCUTS.

1 vol., 12mo. Cloth. . . . . Price, $1.50.

"The entire subject is discussed with a freshness, as well as an elaboration of detail, that renders his work interesting in a more than usual degree. The facts upon which the Darwinian theory is based are presented in an effective manner, conclusions are ably defended, and the question is treated in more compact and available style than in any other work on the same topic that has yet appeared. It is a valuable addition to the 'International Scientific Series.'"—*Boston Post.*

"The present volume is the thirteenth of the 'International Scientific Series,' and is one of the most interesting of all of them. The subject-matter is handled with a great deal of skill and earnestness, and the courage of the author in avowing his opinions is much to his credit. . . . This volume certainly merits a careful perusal."—*Hartford Evening Post.*

"The volume which Prof. Schmidt has devoted to this theme is a valuable contribution to the Darwinian literature. Philosophical in method, and eminently candid, it shows not only the ground which Darwin had in his researches made, and conclusions reached before him to plant his theory upon, but shows, also, what that theory really is, a point upon which many good people who talk very earnestly about the matter are very imperfectly informed."—*Detroit Free Press.*

XIV.

The Chemistry of Light and Photography;

In its Application to Art, Science, and Industry.

By Dr. HERMANN VOGEL,

Professor in the Royal Industrial Academy of Berlin.

WITH 100 ILLUSTRATIONS.

12mo. . . . . Price, $2.00.

"Out of Photography has sprung a new science—the Chemistry of Light—and, in giving a popular view to the one, Dr. Vogel has presented an analysis of the principles and processes of the other. His treatise is as entertaining as it is instructive, pleasantly combining a history of the progress and practice of photography—from the first rough experiments of Wedgwood and Davy with sensitized paper, in 1802, down to the latest improvements of the art—with technical illustrations of the scientific theories on which the art is based. It is the first attempt in any manual of photography to set forth adequately the just claims of the invention, both from an artistic and a scientific point of view, and it must be conceded that the effort has been ably conducted."—*Chicago Tribune.*

D. APPLETON & CO., PUBLISHERS, 549 & 551 Broadway, N. Y.

www.ingramcontent.com/pod-product-compliance
Lightning Source LLC
LaVergne TN
LVHW011221110826
845150LV00006B/1501

* 9 7 8 1 4 2 5 5 1 5 7 8 2 *